SHORT SELLING MASTER

SHORT SELLING MASTER

Proven Strategies from a High-Stakes Day Trader

DAVID CAPABLANCA

Harriman House

HARRIMAN HOUSE
www.harriman-house.com

First published in 2026 by Harriman House, an imprint of Pan Macmillan
EU Representative: Macmillan Publishers Ireland Ltd, 1st Floor, The Liffey Trust Centre, 117-126 Sheriff Street Upper, Dublin 1, D01 YC43
Associated companies throughout the world
www.panmacmillan.com

Paperback ISBN: 978-1-80409-328-3
eBook ISBN: 978-1-80409-329-0
Audio ISBN: 978-1-80409-451-8

British Library Cataloguing in Publication Data
A CIP catalogue record for this book can be obtained from the British Library.

03

Printed and bound by CPI Group (UK) Ltd.

Cover Design by Charlotte Smith. Adobe Stock images used.

CONTENTS

INTRODUCTION

In *Short Selling Master*, I address beginners, intermediates, and expert traders alike who want to explore short selling as a profession. The trading discipline merits the same degree of respect and focus as any entrepreneurial or professional endeavor and involves rigorous study; this is the foundational premise of the book and of my approach to trading.

Short selling has led me to a win ratio of over 90% and seven-figure profits. My strategies, verified multiple times by *Business Insider*, set me apart in an industry in which many hesitate to validate their claims. I don't equivocate; instead, I present proven strategies that lead to profit and financial freedom.

When I first came to trading, I considered long trading; but as I studied short selling, I understood that companies' ultimate goal—boosting their stock prices for survival—creates short-selling opportunities. When stock prices rise sharply in the short term—driven by company press releases, social media campaigns, chat groups, or other promotional channels—the movement often reflects artificially generated demand. These circumstances push prices unjustifiably higher, creating an inflated valuation. Once the hype subsides, prices typically collapse, providing profit opportunities for short sellers. Essentially, traders—and particularly short sellers—can benefit from the inevitable decline of stocks whose prices have been artificially inflated through hype and manipulation.

Once I understood that 'pump-and-dump' chart patterns oftentimes reflect manufactured price spikes that trigger artificial demand and prey on unsuspecting retail traders and investors, I perceived the inequity of that process and dedicated myself to a short-selling approach. The patterns became easily recognizable to me, and I could not reconcile with the fact that nefarious players were pumping and dumping stocks with impunity. I understood that profiting from this practice would be a by-product of bringing balance to the market. I had nothing to lose. Medical bills and student loans had left me submerged in six-figure debt and in need of a high-income skill. At the time, I was attending the master's program in architecture at the University of California, Los Angeles (UCLA)—a pursuit I loved. But six months after my graduation ceremony, in my early 30s, I had to redirect my course of action out of sheer necessity and urgency. I was determined to invest three to five years in becoming profitable and, at 40, reassess if my efforts hadn't panned out by then. In doing so, I had no intention of chasing get-rich-quick schemes—I sought to learn cogent, viable strategies, which would take time and patience.

Over the years, my trading journey became more than a means of financial survival—it evolved into a mission. I committed myself to exposing unethical market practices: pump-and-dump schemes, dubious activity, and the psychological traps that ensnare susceptible traders without the requisite knowledge of the market landscape. To this day, time and again, I witness greed, panic, and a herd mentality fuel market frenzy, from AI booms to electric vehicle hysteria—echoing past financial bubbles.

Successful trading is not about blindly following signals or chasing trends; it's about formulating a strong thesis by understanding why the market moves the way it does and identifying the forces that drive those patterns. This book presents a framework for developing timeless strategies by examining the fundamental and technical forces that shape market behavior. By understanding why trends and news emerge during specific time frames, traders can apply those insights to build effective strategies that extend beyond the examples provided in these pages.

As a short seller, I rely on both fundamental and technical analysis to uncover market movements and patterns, using historical parallels and real-time data to refine my techniques. Once I understand the *why*, I can test and validate my thesis with data and execute with confidence. This approach allows me to adapt and replicate these strategies and techniques ad infinitum.

As an autodidact who never had the benefit of formal training, my aim is to equip aspiring traders with the tools to develop their own strategies like I did—from the ground up, by immersing myself in books, online materials, and videos. Today, I share methodologies that have resonated with me to inspire readers to draw parallels and adopt a personalized approach that aligns with their strengths, insights, and market perspective.

Whether we traders are seeking to refine existing strategies or create entirely new ones, the key is adaptability. The market is constantly evolving and so should our techniques. For years, I approached short selling like a crusader, exposing bad actors and dubious market practices. But today, my focus has shifted. I no longer wear the Batman suit—at least not full time. Instead, I dedicate myself to educating traders about the discipline required to succeed. Trading is not a game. It's not a side hustle. It's a profession demanding countless hours of study, a relentless focus, and an entrepreneurial mindset. Many people equate short selling with gambling, get-rich-quick schemes, or intuition-based trading. None of these assumptions holds true. Short selling is a precise, calculated practice: selling borrowed stock with the expectation of buying it back at a lower price. But that definition barely scratches the surface. This book will walk you through the intricate steps necessary to navigate a market in which the trader failure rate is in the mid to high 90s—not by taking shortcuts, but by employing proven steps toward consistent gains and financial independence.

This book chronicles my trading journey from unusual beginnings: life-threatening circumstances that forced me to reevaluate my slated path, architecture, and immerse myself in the trading discipline—relentlessly and with intense focus—as an autodidact, frontloading countless hours of information that would typically take high-powered investment firm recruits a few years to learn. Each chapter contains stories from my trading experiences and what these experiences taught me. Budding and seasoned traders alike can apply these 'Lessons learned' to their own trading odysseys.

I came to realize that one single trade can threaten your staying power in the market—or worse, leave you with nothing. However, I hit upon a winning formula: rigorous study, tenacity, and the right approach to the trading discipline are the antidotes to ruin.

Along the way, I made mistakes. I learned to navigate a highly volatile market, in which uncertainty is a way of life; but by journaling, employing incisive techniques and strategies, and developing the mindset of a trader, I positioned myself according to my stringent rules with the goal of avoiding most 'black swan' events—unexpected, blind-siding occurrences that can have a devastating impact on one's entire trading career.

To complement the 'Lessons learned,' I offer 'A word to the wise' sections—intermittent commentaries about specific trading scenarios that can cause confusion or misunderstanding. These concise collections of practical suggestions, guiding principles, cautionary reminders, and actionable advice are all derived from real-life trading experiences.

At the end of each chapter, I also include a 'Tips and Tricks' section, which distills pragmatic, high-impact insights from each chapter into guidance that traders can apply instantly. By the end of our journey, readers will have an in-depth understanding of how to analyze market movements, identify profitable opportunities, and develop a strategic mindset that leads to confident, incisive market strategies. The goal is not just to follow trends but to anticipate them, adapt to them, and then act out of knowledge and discernment, not greed and panic.

The secret is to look before you leap; refrain from rushing to judgment and acting on temptation; and above all, use the past as a guidepost for every move you make. By paying attention to history, we hold up a mirror to ourselves; and with effort and determination, we can reach the zenith of our potential.

Chapter 1

BURNING THE BOATS

In this chapter, I recount my journey into short selling and my motivations for short selling paid promotions. I discuss the definition of 'short selling,' the historical impact of market bubbles, and how they relate to trading in today's market. Readers will learn how to react to market uncertainty—especially beginners with margin accounts who may potentially encounter rare, unexpected 'black swan' events—and how to turn losses into lessons. In addition, beginners will learn the significance of overcoming the pattern day trade (PDT) rule, which guards against excessive risk-taking and potential wipeout.

CHALLENGES ARE INTEGRAL TO THE JOURNEY

One lesson I learned at the outset of my trading journey is that life is full of unexpected twists and turns that challenge your resolve. Success isn't about chance; it's about relentless effort, focus, and the courage to embrace both victory and defeat as integral parts of the journey. Take it from me—the survivor of a five-centimeter brain tumor, excised during a 20-hour operation when I was just 25.

When my medical and student loans fell due, reality hit me like a ton of bricks. Had I continued to pursue my intended course, my love of the art and science of architecture would have been subsumed by the pressures associated with my debt. I'd have lived paycheck to paycheck indefinitely and would have been unable to work at my optimum in my chosen field. My career shift toward a high-income skill paved the way to a more financially secure future. The only constant in life is change and navigating this unpredictable path requires preparedness—of mind, body, and soul. Like the stock market, life demands that you embrace the unexpected as an ally, seeing it as an opportunity to grow beyond your limits.

From this perspective, I began studying short selling with the same rigor and discipline I had once applied to my architectural studies. In pursuing an education like a college student, I entered the trading world as a *tabula rasa*—a blank slate, eager to absorb and learn.

Even the world's smartest people can't figure out the market. Intelligence, education, and erudition do not equate to successful trading. Intellect and academic knowhow don't translate into market wizardry. Some professionals (e.g., doctors, lawyers, architects) experience failure in the trading discipline, which humbles them quickly. They don't know it all; no one does. I defeated the odds by sheer force of will—the compulsion to become a sponge and cram thousands of hours into a brief timespan. I had no alternative, no Plan B.

This urgency was my foundational impetus and was key to my success as I voluntarily charted an unconventional course, retreating from society and socialization to become an autodidact. I studied thousands of hours of trading materials, literature, and videos, completely immersing myself in the world of short selling to the negation of all other interests and preoccupations. Essentially, I 'burned the boats,' like Hernán Cortés and the Spanish conquistadors who, in 1519, on the shores of present-day Mexico, burned their boats, effectively cutting off any possibility of retreat. That bold move forced Cortés and his troops to fully commit to their mission, symbolizing a point of no return.

But I digress.

'What is short selling?' you want to know. Good question.

WHAT IS SHORT SELLING?

For the uninitiated, short selling involves borrowing a stock's shares from a broker and selling them at the current market price. Later, if the stock price drops, the short seller can buy the shares back at the lower price, return them to the broker, and pocket the difference as profit. However, if the price rises instead, the short seller must buy back at a higher price, resulting in a loss.

I didn't even know this definition when I started out on my journey in 2016. I had miles to travel; but by acknowledging my lack of knowledge, I freed myself to explore, learn, and reinvent myself as a short-selling master.

It's important to note that short selling is inherently riskier than going long because a stock's potential losses are theoretically unlimited, as prices can rise infinitely. In contrast, when going long, the maximum loss is limited to the initial investment, as prices can only fall to zero.

An essential aspect of short selling is the ability to apply both fundamental and technical analysis.

FUNDAMENTAL ANALYSIS

Fundamental analysis involves reviewing the skeletons in a company's closet to understand its backstory. In doing so, I consider questions like the following:

- What is the company's cash need?
- What forms of dilution does the company have and which underwriters were involved with the given dilution?
- Who owns the warrants and/or convertibles?

- Is the company in need of cash? How much cash runway does it have left?
- What kinds of products does the company make and in what industry does it operate?
- Tying this back to the overall market environment, are the S&P, Nasdaq, and Dow climbing or falling?
- Is there a global event, such as a war or the like, that I need to be aware of?

TECHNICAL ANALYSIS

For a short seller, technical analysis involves high stakes in an extremely volatile environment, where stocks can move hundreds or thousands of percentage points a day. It's dangerous; but if you have the correct strategies in play, the landscape is very manageable, demanding rigorous concentration and in-depth assessment.

Technical analysis involves the indicators that charts produce. You must ask, 'What is the chart saying?' The chart is a representation of the people behind it (i.e., buyers and sellers).

With stocks, you have the advantage of constantly recurring patterns and you must be prepared to analyze them. For example, certain candlestick formations are prime for short selling, and you must be able to recognize them to capture the exact moment at which to enter a trade.

If you don't know what patterns to observe and how to spot them—if you proceed by fundamentals alone—you will get squeezed by the stock manipulation of dubious companies (pumps). In the realm of short selling, the term 'pump and dump' signifies that the stocks have been artificially inflated through hype, manipulation, or false information (pump), and will thus inevitably—and sometimes precipitously—decline (dump), due to their unsustainable nature. You have to look at where you are in the big picture of pump and dumps—as in baseball, which inning you're in affects the significance of events.

A word to the wise

Pump-and-dump manipulations are rampant online. They often lure unsuspecting individuals through newsletters with enticing keywords like 'hot stocks' or 'get rich quick.' Hidden in the fine print of these promotions are disclaimers revealing that third parties have paid exorbitant sums for these campaigns to offload their holdings onto unsuspecting buyers. The stocks are pumped up by artificial demand and then dumped, leaving retail investors with worthless shares.

HISTORY DOESN'T REPEAT ITSELF, BUT IT OFTEN RHYMES

Mark Twain's famous quote has resonance with regard to the stock market: "History doesn't repeat itself, but it often rhymes." A glimpse at history reveals recurring patterns in the market—clues about the behavior and movement of stocks. Such patterns are particularly interesting for short sellers. I immersed myself in fundamental and technical analysis to obtain a panoramic view of the stock market.

It's important to determine where we are within the framework of history. Human nature is immutable. We remain the same throughout time; we just wear different clothes. A glance at history reveals that chart patterns often reflect human behavior. For example, there have been a series of manias, or market bubbles, that have grown and burst throughout the centuries; and although the market eventually recovers, it is important to be able to identify the cause of these surges and crashes. People put money in the market believing that stocks will keep rising and take out credit to indulge in materialism. The false assumption is that the party will continue. As these euphoric individuals keep their money in the stock market and watch it increase, they think they are affluent. But this is a complete delusion because they haven't cashed out yet. They live under the illusion that there is ample money in their accounts and spend above their means as though that were the case. Then they take out loans on credit because to them, it's a no-brainer: the market will give them a higher percentage return than the negative rate against their borrowed money.

So, Joe Q. Public takes out a loan and puts the money in the market without ever considering that a crash may be on the way. Periods of exuberant prosperity can last for more than a decade—as occurred in the Roaring Twenties, which culminated abruptly on Black Tuesday (October 29, 1929). At that time, the Dow dropped 12%, obliterating billions of dollars of wealth. This is a classic sign of a market bubble: human greed—the nature of the beast. Where there is an opportunity to manipulate the market, people will seize it as if it were the Holy Grail.

In other words, pump and dumps are classic strategies. I short sell them, first looking to the past to evaluate what types of companies are involved. Interestingly, the pump-and-dump stocks of the past look identical to those that I short in the present. Studying precedent gives me greater confidence in my analyses. That is a strategy in and of itself: I get a glimpse of the future by analyzing the past, which becomes an indicator of what will happen in the future. Whether we are dealing with paid promotions, reverse splits, or patent plays, they all follow the same pattern of pump and dumps: surges and crashes.

History also demonstrates the markets' inherent unpredictability. One frequently quoted phrase in the industry cautions us that: "The market can remain irrational longer than you can remain solvent." That is, prices in financial markets don't always reflect underlying value or logic. They can swing irrationally based on herd behavior, speculation, hype, fear, or randomness. This irrationality can last far longer than you might expect. When shorting pump and dumps, keep in mind that they can continue going up longer than you think—sometimes for weeks or months. That is why my process is so important—specifically, my identification of stocks that inevitably will crash within certain time frames when I decide to enter my initial position. I dive into these in-depth strategies in the pages that follow.

History doesn't repeat itself, but it often rhymes. Market trends are not always identical, so we must use our imagination to see the parallels. Once traders understand this, they can prepare themselves for the next crash by seeing the storm coming. If they perceive an impending crash, they can be prepared to have cash to buy (or, in my case, be prepared to short the stock).

Everything in the market is counterintuitive. In stressful, volatile times, the world seems apocalyptic, in an end-of-days phase. Fear drives market prices down, panic ensues, and "there's blood in the streets," as Warren Buffett (per British financier Baron Rothschild) observes. That is the time to buy, but traders must fight their intuition to do so—a learned trait.

WHY SHORT SELLING?

This understanding of market behavior resonated with me. When I started out, I had a chip on my shoulder because I saw people acquiring wealth through manipulation while I was struggling to pivot from architecture. I thought that by shifting careers I was being compelled to abandon a life and professional trajectory I loved. In truth, however, that transformation was an extension of who I had been as an aspiring architect, and I quickly learned that trading—like architecture—is both an art and a science.

At first, the charts appeared highly complex. However, once someone explained the pump-and-dump schemes and the so-called 'walk-ups'—a form of price manipulation integral to constructing a pump and dump's fragile house of cards—it became clear how manipulators like Jordan Belfort, the infamous Wolf of Wall Street, exploited these tactics. Belfort was the protagonist of the 2007 film of the same name starring Leonardo DiCaprio, which chronicled his deceptive practices. I gained an advantage by understanding the end game: the stock would inevitably crash and the manipulators would cash out. That knowledge gave me an edge. Then, I had to gain awareness of how far a stock could potentially run. For that reason, I traded small-size for a couple of years with specific stocks, learning the timeless strategy of the pump-and-dump cycle. I still stick to that strategy, with little variation.

The small-cap market (stocks with a market cap of less than $250 million) is more volatile, and volatile stocks provide the opportunity for account growth (hence my focus on small-caps). As a short seller, I don't thrive on driving stock prices down, as some erroneously believe. On the contrary, I want to be a thorn in the side of these dubious actors. We who seek to stop them most likely won't succeed completely, but we can give them a hard time.

As I told my Delta Chi Fraternity on a trip back to my alma mater, the University of Florida, in September 2024: "Through mentorship and education, we can stand on the shoulders of history and make a mark in the world and in our personal lives." Also, when we augment our financial decision-making with short selling, we gain access to the mental processes of long sellers and the yin-yang relationship between the two. Chapter 11 delves further into this concept.

HISTORICAL FRAMEWORK: LESSONS FROM MARKET BUBBLES

My exploration of history led me to study market bubbles—dramatic episodes of euphoria and collapse that reveal the immutable underpinnings of human behavior. These historical moments, though separated by centuries, share striking similarities, driven by overvaluation, speculation, and easy access to liquidity.

One key example is the speculative tulip market bubble that occurred during the Dutch Golden Age in the 17th century, when these flowers became all the rage—until a major auction failed and panic set in, causing severe market instability. Similarly, the South Sea Bubble surfaced in 1720, when Sir Isaac Newton invested in the stock market and chased the top due to fear of missing out (FOMO). Reflecting on the disaster, Newton famously stated: "I can calculate the motions of the heavenly bodies, but not the madness of men." Intelligence and success in the market do not necessarily go hand in hand.

During the Roaring Twenties, Joe Kennedy—the patriarch of the American political dynasty—consistently coordinated pump-and-dump schemes with the big players, causing ordinary people to lose money while the rich grew richer. Anecdote has it that just before the crash, he decided to sell his stock holdings after receiving tips from a shoeshine boy, which he believed was a sign that the market had become overly speculative. Hence the quote: "You know it's time to sell when even the shoeshine boys are giving you stock tips." This suggests that when casual observers find themselves swept up in a stock market frenzy, speculation has gone mainstream. When the shoeshine boys are mentioning this, there is usually no one left to buy. This means that some measure of selling can lead to a panic and consequent market crash.

More recent bubbles include the dot-com crash at the turn of the millennium and the global financial crisis of 2008. Lured by visions of unprecedented growth, investors disregarded market fundamentals, leading to speculative investments, inflated valuations, and devastating portfolios. All these economic disasters have three things in common that have never changed over time:

1. **Overvaluation:** A situation in which people overvalue companies based on potential future earnings rather than current value.
2. **Speculation:** A high level of speculation and investment in unproven business models.
3. **Liquidity:** Easy access to capital and investment funds. People thought they had nothing to lose, but they were deluded.

ASSIMILATION IN A MARKET OF UNCERTAINTY

So how did I factor into the mix, weighed down by student and medical debt, in addition to my social conditioning about what the world expected of me? Well, I had to take a leap—but not *that* far. As I researched and studied trading, I decided to liberate myself from life's baggage, mental clutter, and surrounding distractions and essentially return to student mode. When I was an undergraduate at the University of Florida, I pursued my passion—architecture—with unwavering focus, and I wanted to do the same with trading. As much as I loved my initially chosen discipline, it would take another three years to obtain my architecture license, and I would have to earn a subpar salary until then. This was not a viable course of action if I wanted to achieve financial stability. So, amid whispers of negativity, I resolved to stick to my new career trajectory with unflagging determination.

My classmates spoke their minds. "What's happened to David? He's left architecture! He must have gone crazy after his brain surgery." I heard these judgmental opinions through the grapevine and, as hurtful as they were, they simultaneously drove me to pursue my objectives with greater determination.

At that point, other aspects of my world began to implode. I was in over my head financially and side jobs were crucial to make ends meet. I spent six months as an Uber driver to pay for my online stock courses, amounting to $7,000 (a small fortune from my perspective). During my first couple of years as a trader, I gradually invested an additional $2,500 in stock-related educational materials, including books and audiobooks. I became obsessed with gathering and unearthing knowledge. When one credible source mentioned another, I went on to study that second source; and when that second source referred to a third, I delved into it with fervor and continued journeying down the rabbit hole.

Sometimes I converted my driver's seat into a bed and didn't return home, seeking to avoid my landlord's tirades and earn nominal daily amounts to keep my head above water. I had to prioritize my dream; I could not rest unless I did. In my mind, everything else was subordinate to that goal.

Naturally, I faced stumbling blocks, which I confronted head-on. Since much of the information shared online about the trading industry is unverified, a lot of false information is floating around out there in the ether to attract unsuspecting novices. Therefore, it is important only to look for traders with verifiable track records—those that have been verified multiple times by credible trading sources. Authenticity is paramount.

Anyone can claim to be versed in the subject matter without a verified track record. These individuals are not "gurus," but "furus" (i.e., fake gurus, without substance or foundation). I was aware of and profoundly anxious about these 'furus' who threatened to derail me entirely if I did not research all my study materials thoroughly before I paid for them. I was in my mid-30s, without a moment to squander. Every move, every thought, every cent was invested in doing the right thing so I could take my best shot at trading success. As I strived to achieve my goal, I tried to avoid all the misinformation and disinformation, while simultaneously honing my work ethic and determination—the core elements for reaching the pinnacle of prosperity and perhaps even achieving millionaire trader status.

In my mind—and in reality—I felt that everyone was against my decision, even people I met casually. I once accepted an Uber passenger while studying a stock-trading audiobook. The gentleman didn't seem to mind and I continued to play the audiobook during the ride. When we reached our destination, the passenger deigned to speak to me: "You've got to stop listening to that, man! You're going to lose all your money. It's a scam!" My passenger thought his advice would be helpful, but he only added to the chorus of negativity I was desperately trying to avoid.

A word to the wise

Pursuing a non-traditional path invites skepticism and criticism. However, staying true to your vision, even in the face of societal judgment, underscores the importance of self-belief and purpose.

TRANSFORMATION

While I was driving for Uber, I also took on tutoring jobs to cover my rent. Drawing on the knowledge I had amassed as an architecture student, I taught every conceivable subject—math, science, arts—and established a credible reputation. The jobs paid $50–$100 an hour, two to three hours a day, about three days a week. I had to cover all my expenses as I continued to live a minimalist life, devoting myself exclusively to stock trading. I made significantly more from tutoring than I had earned in architecture, and I had fun mentoring my students and watching them soak up information. I did well, and my tutoring skills were in such high demand that I had to turn down jobs to focus on my studies.

Part-time tutoring gave me the time and space to organize my schedule and regroup, but it did not solve all my debt issues. Rather, I required exponential growth through a high-income skill and stock trading was my ultimate path forward. I had a vision and a plan, which I executed with steely resolve. I listened to and analyzed the methodologies of renowned experts in the field who fueled my enthusiasm and dove into the history of trends since the late 1990s. I learned about C-suite moguls and company employees, joined the dots, and tried to solve the puzzle of artificially inflated stocks. I did not solely wish to navigate the market and explore the ins and outs; I wanted to master it entirely.

Eventually, the Uber driving faded away; as did the grunt work that I had secured through architecture. I was drained but more at peace, having established a following in my tutoring circles. At one point, the company I worked for offered me a partnership in the franchise, but I was so engrossed in learning about stocks that I turned down the opportunity. Had I accepted their offer, I would still be in my financial debt predicament, and I had to think pragmatically.

In focusing entirely on my chosen objective, I recalled my days as an undergraduate architecture student at the University of Florida. There, we adhered to what we called 'studio culture,' which focused on working single-mindedly at a given task. I wanted to simulate that methodology, and that meant I needed to dedicate every waking moment to my new discipline, free of all distractions. There were not enough hours in the day to absorb the depth and scope of material. It is not hyperbole to state that I had to cram 20 years of work into a tiny fraction of that time to build expertise and standing in the trading industry.

In doing so, I transformed every aspect of my life—I sold my car, changed my number, and essentially isolated myself from society (including close family members and friends). I was not, by nature, an isolationist; I simply knew that to achieve the highest level of expertise in short selling, I had to renounce materialism and personal indulgences. Therefore, I retreated into my own microcosm of relentless study of the trading discipline. I rented a shared office space in the U.S. Bank Tower with a desk and a strong Wi-Fi signal for about $200 a month, and I slept on the floor there, with my jacket serving as a pillow. That was the only way I could secure my financial future.

I decided on a high-probability approach to trading: shorting paid promotions. The pattern of these stocks was easy to spot. Stocks would surge without rhyme or reason for days or weeks, then inevitably crash. Stock manipulators in 'boiler rooms'—high-pressure, speculative, or worthless sales operations run by stock manipulators seeking to circumvent the law and lure in unsuspecting buyers—would manipulate (pump) the stock and entice innocent investors with an exciting promotion. Today, that might be AI or quantum computing—anything that seems like the 'hot' theme of the day. Manipulators capitalize on human greed, which has always been their modus operandi. In the 1920s, this was perpetrated through word of mouth; by the 1980s and 1990s, the telephone had become the preferred mode of communication; and today, the schemers' methodology variously encompasses computers, text messages, message boards, chatrooms, and social media, rendering the former methods obsolete. Even the most grounded professionals can be susceptible to that ubiquitous emotion, avarice, and can fall for the pattern of a gradual uptrend. Inevitably, however, with nothing to sustain the price, the stock will fall like a house of cards.

As a beginner with little to no guidance, I felt comfortable taking a defensive position and growing my account steadily through high-conviction pump-and-dump strategies. From 2015 to 2018, this was a reliable approach. These days, however, purposeful squeezes occur—that is, prices rise instead of falling and short sellers are forced to cover their positions faster to avoid potential outlier losses. The market is an ever-evolving construct, and you must learn to adapt accordingly.

THE PATTERN DAY TRADE RULE

An essential lesson I learned from my losses was the need to overcome the PDT rule. The rule—which applies only to US-based traders—was established in 2001 in the aftermath of the dot-com boom and bust, during which many investors suffered significant financial losses.

In response, the Securities and Exchange Commission (SEC) introduced the PDT rule to protect traders by restricting frequent day trading among less-experienced investors. (Day trades are purchases or sales of securities on the same trading day.) The rule requires day traders (i.e., those who execute more than three day trades in a margin account within five business days) to maintain a $25,000 account at minimum. This facilitates unlimited day trades. Failure to maintain the requisite amount results in a prohibition on further trades until the account is compliant.

A trader who engages in more than three trades in a five-day period will be issued a first-time warning. A second transgression will result in 90 days of restricted access to trades. Essentially, the Financial Industry Regulatory Authority established the PDT rule to shield investors from their own recklessness. Without the appropriate education about trading and its benefits and pitfalls, the market can swallow up unwitting investors, leaving them without recourse. Thus, although the PDT rule is outdated ($25,000 had a much higher value when the rule was introduced than it does today), it still helps to mitigate the human propensity to leap without looking.

A BLACK SWAN SCENARIO

My rigorous study, research, and trial-and-error strategies over several years suggested that pump and dumps were largely immune to 'black swan' scenarios—rare, highly unpredictable events that can cause extreme disruption in financial markets. (Nassim Taleb popularized the term in his book *The Black Swan*, discussed further below.)

No amount of data could prepare me for such an unprecedented event, and I was in for a rude awakening. In February 2020, the Covid-19 pandemic plunged the world into uncertainty. Soon thereafter, people found themselves unemployed, sequestered at home, trading on their computers and devices. When news came out that biotechnology company CytoDyn Inc. (CYDY)—an over-the-counter (OTC) stock, not listed on the exchanges—had developed treatments for HIV, cancer, and autoimmune diseases, the altruistic desire to save the world, however well-meaning, obliterated all need for caution. A frenzy ensued, which exhibited all the characteristics of a market bubble.

Despite my awareness that my margin account limited me to three day trades within a five-day period, I shorted CYDY. Then, over the weekend, a news network aired a paid segment about a lifesaving patient-tested treatment for Covid-19. I held the stock as a swing trade. Swing trading is a strategy used to capitalize on short- to medium-term profits in stocks, commodities, or other financial instruments over a period of days to weeks. Swing traders typically hold positions longer than day traders, who close out positions at the end of each trading day, but shorter than investors, who may hold for months or years.

I anticipated a crash, but the price surged precipitously amid considerable hype. On Monday morning, unable to exit at the premarket open (1 a.m. PST), I anxiously covered my position at $3.50 and incurred a loss of $11,000—the equivalent of a year's worth of net gains up to that point. From 2015, the outset of my journey, until this 'black swan' event in 2020, I had only traded paid pump and dumps, which was the highest-probability setup that I knew and felt comfortable with trading at the time. Up until CYDY, my accounts had shown hopeful signs of overcoming PDT organically and had grown exponentially without the limitations of day trades. I had been generally profitable with small wins over time. I viewed this interval of time as a learning experience, not a money-making endeavor. I was relieved that I never lost money. I did not rely on the money in my account; I just wanted to make incremental progress. Therefore, although the loss was devastating, it did not derail me altogether.

While I felt as though I had attended a funeral after the CYDY debacle, I was determined to keep moving toward my goals. Despite my despondency, I knew this wouldn't be my first uphill battle. With limited funds, I relied on a slow, methodical strategy, shorting paid pump promotions and applying the knowledge gleaned from my voluminous research materials. Michael Marcus—the first trader featured in Jack D. Schwager's *Market Wizards*, who took a decade to become profitable—was an inspiration; as was Seth, an expert trader in Puerto Rico whose trading videos I discovered on YouTube. Although I did not know Seth personally at the time, he became my chosen mentor. His deep insight impressed me and I studied his videos repeatedly, envisioning myself in his office, rubbing elbows with the most seasoned, successful traders.

CYDY would later surge to $10 in June 2020 amid continued hype, so my early exit allowed me to preserve enough funds to keep trading. That decision, though painful, ensured I could continue my journey and avoid complete ruin. From then on, I adopted the philosophy that no single trade was worth my career.

A word to the wise

During market bubbles, short sellers open themselves up to increased risk exposure by holding stocks short overnight. Desperate companies in need of cash which operate outside the sectors involved in the bubble somehow find a way to inject themselves into the fray and ride the coattails of the stocks that are part of the frenzy.

TURNING LOSS INTO A FOUNDATIONAL GROWTH LESSON

The CYDY fiasco was a lesson in respecting the market's unpredictability and prioritizing the preservation of my trading account above all else. This philosophy served me well throughout the chaotic market conditions that followed, reinforcing my ultimate objective: trading is not just about profit but also *longevity*, and I was determined to devote myself to that wholeheartedly.

My swing trade on CYDY taught me that shorting overnight in a volatile market was a recipe for disaster. Biotech stocks, often driven by hype and speculation, preyed on pandemic-related hype to artificially inflate their value. As I had only narrowly escaped penury, I realized the necessity of adapting my strategy. Swing trading was no longer viable in this environment. Instead, I needed to focus on intraday trades and maintain flexibility.

Determined to turn my loss into a lesson, I read Nassim Taleb's *The Black Swan*—a seminal work that defines 'black swans' as highly unpredictable events for which traders should nonetheless prepare by managing risk in various spheres of life, especially in circumstances where volatility exists. The author encourages robust decision-making to promote awareness of traditional risk assessment models and highlights the importance of diversity in mitigating the potential losses occasioned by such occurrences.

I also found solace in books like David Goggins' *Can't Hurt Me*, which chronicles the author's journey from childhood poverty and abuse to supreme success as an endurance athlete and Navy SEAL, inspiring me to push beyond perceived limits. Mike Bellafiore's *The Playbook: An Inside Look at How to Think Like a Professional Trader* also had a profound impact and pointed me to the story of Hernán Cortés, mentioned earlier.

In addition, I devoured the audiobook of Bellafiore's *One Good Trade: Inside the Highly Competitive World of Proprietary Trading*, which a prominent trader highly recommended to me.

I also delved into Steve Nison's *Japanese Candlestick Charting Techniques: A Contemporary Guide to the Ancient Investment Techniques of the Far East*, which introduced these charting methods to Western traders.

LESSONS LEARNED

My early loss taught me vital lessons that enabled me to move forward on my trading journey. Specifically, I focused on the following.

THE BEHAVIOR OF OTC STOCKS

OTC stocks do not trade premarket or after hours like Nasdaq or New York Stock Exchange (NYSE) listed stocks. Listed stocks trade premarket from 4 a.m. to 9:30 a.m. EST and after hours, 4 p.m. to 8 p.m. EST, offering some exit opportunities with reduced liquidity.

AVOIDING 'HOT' SECTORS IN UNCERTAIN TIMES

In times of uncertainty, avoid shorting 'hot' sectors. Particularly during a pandemic, biotech stocks like CYDY create a frenzy, draw speculative interest, and tug at people's emotions, leading to extreme volatility.

Taking the pandemic as an example, car companies might purport to produce ventilators; while cleaning companies might claim they had a surplus of Clorox, which helps to kill the Covid-19 virus. Any company could pop out of the woodwork with baseless allegations and cause a stock to surge overnight by hundreds or even thousands of percentage points. That is a devastating scenario for a short seller, who may be virtually obliterated in the process. Therefore, it's wise not to short overnight in such an environment.

THE IMPORTANCE OF OVERCOMING THE PDT RULE

The key takeaway: the market can remain irrational longer than a trader can remain solvent. Again, understanding and overcoming the PDT rule and better capitalizing my account were critical to achieving the freedom to trade without these limitations.

TIPS AND TRICKS

- **Stick to a high-probability strategy**: Begin with a single, high-probability strategy and master it before exploring others. When I started out, I chose to short sell paid promotions, which presented a manageable learning curve, reduced risk, enhanced predictability, and were easy to spot. This setup presented the best win-ratio, revealed through back-testing at the time, and still works to this day.

- **Trade small size—sometimes under 100 shares**: I recommend opening a minimum margin account ($2,000) and risking 10% to have 'skin in the game.' In this way, you have money on the line (as opposed to paper trading, which does not provide the same feeling of involvement). Just keep the account moving in the right direction without risking too much. If you make a mistake, you can still come back without being wiped out. Remember that your greatest vulnerability arises as a beginner. Therefore, it is important to proceed slowly and incrementally.
- **Begin slowly and judiciously**: Self-educate by reading books like this one, listening to podcasts like *The Friendly Bear*, and studying rigorously. The PDT rule is a blessing in disguise. Although it requires you to keep at least $25,000 in your account if you want to day trade frequently, it prevents you from over-trading recklessly and encourages you to look before you leap. A gradual approach is essential to longevity and is analogous to an entrepreneurial venture. If a business owner overcapitalizes and proceeds too quickly, they may take a huge loss from which they cannot recover. Also, remember that the past is prologue—history serves as a benchmark for future trends and opportunities. Examine the market bubbles discussed in this chapter and understand the chart patterns, which are visual representations of human nature—the propensity for fear and susceptibility to hype and greed.
- **Manage risk relentlessly**: Never risk ruin. Avoid volatile sectors and overexposure to black swan events.
- **Embrace the journey**: Success in trading is a long-term pursuit. Don't focus on instant gratification and view setbacks not as losses, but as opportunities for growth.

Chapter 2

EVOLUTION OF A SHORT SELLER

IN THIS CHAPTER, I revisit my encounters with meme stocks—specifically Super League Enterprise, Inc. (formerly Super League Gaming, Inc.) (SLGG)—while still trading in the premarket with considerable success. Without the refined skills of a seasoned day trader, I withstood another substantial loss in a frenzied market environment. Although this loss was painful, I learned the importance of defensive trading and journaling my process, including my mistakes. Most significantly, I never gave up. Instead, I learned how to trade defensively in a market rife with speculation and herd behavior. Learning from my mistakes reinforced my disciplined approach and helped fuel my desire to rebound and continue my journey. My ultimate takeaway: challenges are fleeting, and with a healthy dose of determination, tenacity, and envisioning, your objectives will manifest.

THE SIGNIFICANCE OF OBSERVING THE MARKET

With $5,000 remaining in my account, I gathered an additional $24,000 to amass a total of $29,000 (thus overcoming the PDT rule).

I watched the market and pulled all-nighters, continuing to study diligently. During the premarket (4 a.m. EST, which was 1 a.m. PST in Los Angeles), as most people slept, I witnessed abnormal surges in volume. Pandemic-related stocks (mostly biotechs, pharmaceuticals, and other medically geared companies) would gap up hundreds, sometimes thousands of percent and then slowly fade back down. I would short these, but very few brokerages allowed these stocks to be traded at the 4 a.m. EST premarket open, as the premarket volume in 2020 was unprecedented and few brokers were equipped to trade that early. However, my direct-access broker allowed me to trade at that time. During this period, only direct-access brokers were available for trading, which caused erratic liquidity as the demand for stocks remained low until the larger brokerages opened.

NAVIGATING A NEW FRONTIER

With volume and liquidity increasing to record levels during the pandemic, premarket trading was a new frontier. I just happened to be on the frontlines at the right time. Big traders were asleep; Wall Street was closed; hedge fund traders were still out of the office. But I was there, awake, alert, and paying attention, with just enough knowledge to take advantage of the state of the market. In September 2020, when I gazed at the $10,000 profit in my account, it looked like fairy dust—mere numbers on a screen. It was hard for me to believe that this was *actual money*, and that the strategy I was employing in the premarket was viable and real. So, I undertook every trade defensively, hyper-vigilantly, trying to avert another loss. I derived all my gains from my premarket strategies, mostly in the first hour. Observing the market is an essential part of a trader's learning process. However, I knew that I couldn't solely trade the premarket forever. Eventually, I would have to trade regular hours if I wanted to become fully self-sufficient and evolve as a trader.

By late September 2020, when my account had grown from $29,000 to $50,000, I was still only trading premarket. My peers thought I was crazy, but the strategy worked for me—one trade at a time. As we moved into October 2020, I noticed that the premarket had slowed down and opportunities had evaporated. As a novice, I had yet to discover that the market moves in volatile cycles, especially in the presence of uncertainty (caused by the pandemic at the time). So, without knowing what would occur in the foreseeable future, I took time off to recalibrate mentally and travel to South America.

Upon my return in late January 2021, I immersed myself once again in the market, which was now gripped by the meme stock phenomenon (emblematic of the market bubbles of the past—another pump and dump). Fueled by social media platforms like Reddit, stocks such as GameStop (GME) and AMC Entertainment (AMC) soared to absurd valuations as the crowd targeted and bought these stocks en masse to squeeze out the short sellers involved.

AMC experienced a surge in popularity among people at home from work due to Covid-19. Individuals traded on their devices with money they received from stimulus checks—funds they perceived to be expendable. Everyone was trading on their phones, iPads, and computers, obsessed with Robinhood—a popular trading app named for the legendary folk hero who robbed from the rich and gave to the poor. This emotionally charged environment created the perfect framework for me, as I was equipped with the necessary preparation and knowledge to seize the opportunities amid the frenzy.

Although many traders flocked to Robinhood, with its sleek design and gamified interface, the app offered limited tools and features, including no access to short selling; and in addition, it only opened at 9 a.m. EST. It seemed almost designed for novice traders to fail. In contrast, I was equipped with a direct-access broker, providing full capabilities, including early 4 a.m. EST premarket trading and a comprehensive suite of tools that set me up for success. In their fervor, the novice traders based their actions on rumors and groundless assertions they encountered on the internet and simply followed the crowd. Harking back to Tulip Mania, the South Sea Bubble, the Roaring Twenties, and the dot-com boom, I understood that following the conformists was not advisable. Over 5,000 study hours up to that point had taught me that reward in these scenarios is transitory; inevitably, panic would set in and the meme stocks would subsequently crash.

Against the backdrop of this hysteria, I also encountered SLGG, which came to my attention on March 3, 2020. SLGG was a small gaming entertainment company without capital, based in Santa Monica, California. At 4 a.m. EST, the stock was dormant; but by 7 a.m. EST, it was rising. "What is happening?" I asked myself. "Is this randomness, or is something happening that I'm unaware of?" My process wasn't as refined as it is today, so I didn't pause to research the company. I was still honing my skills, and all I knew was that the environment was frenetic.

SPECULATION AD RIDICULUM

Amid the fray, I saw a post on Twitter (now X) by Ryan Cohen, the activist investor and eventual CEO of GME: a potentially cryptic message featuring a frog emoji and an ice cream cone. Immediately, the market went wild. The LinkedIn profile of SLGG CEO Ann Hand revealed that in 1999 she had worked for McDonald's, which sold soft-serve ice cream cones. Her profile also indicated that she had been the CEO of Project Frog—a company that designs and develops prefabricated building systems and components to streamline the construction process—before joining SLGG in 2015. As people scoured the internet, trying frantically to find a correlation between the emojis in Cohen's post and stocks, someone came up with the speculative supposition that GME intended to acquire SLGG. There was no sound evidentiary basis for believing this would happen, but people were not thinking logically—they just invented a meaningless narrative. Nothing made sense. People simply followed a groundless theory like flocks of sheep.

The incident taught me that high demand (i.e., volume) is synonymous with mania and hysteria; and that traders can learn how to recognize such an environment, characterized by heightened emotion—fear and greed. Everyone wanted to get their hands on the latest hot stock and believed SLGG would be the next AMC, which squeezed hundreds of percentage points. They thought, 'What if SLGG is what Ryan Cohen was referring to with his emojis and GME is going to acquire it?' Even the most educated of these investors (e.g., lawyers, doctors, and other professionals) wanted to become involved. The emojis were enough to spark a rumor, which in turn caused an exponential spike in demand.

IN THE PATH OF A FREIGHT TRAIN

Although I understood the climate, I was still relatively inexperienced, yet I nonetheless put myself in the path of a freight train, hoping to ride it out. While the crowd—Cohen's stampeding sheep—went long (i.e., they bought the stock), I was one of the few short sellers in the path. I closed the trade on March 5, 2020 and took a $19,000 loss. I journaled my experience, tried to learn from it as much as possible, and discovered that millions of sheep can overrun anything in their wake. The crowd's reaction was a classic example of the market bubbles of the past.

Massive pump-and-dump schemes, like those perpetuated by media hype, invariably result in a devastating crash, engendering resentment and bitterness. When the house of cards folds, life savings vanish, marriages fail, and relationships in all spheres suffer.

This experience reinforced the importance of avoiding the herd mentality and sticking to a disciplined approach. I quickly recovered my losses and continued to grow my account, which had already reached six figures by this point.

My takeaway: the power of envisioning and self-assessment.

My ability to recover from losses and move in the direction of my goals came with great attention to discipline in every aspect of my life, including my personal hygiene. During the pandemic, the local gyms and hotels had closed due to lockdown, and I couldn't shower there; so, I had to resort to showering on Skid Row. Wearing a poker face for protection in that dangerous neighborhood, I hurriedly walked the 15-minute distance from my office and returned for the premarket open at 1 a.m. PST (4 a.m. EST). I even shaved my head to avoid having to wash my hair in the limited time I had to shower. I told myself that such experiences were transitory. Like life, the market is in constant flux.

A word to the wise

The Covid-19 pandemic was a unique time in history, presenting daily opportunities amid high volatility and a forgiving market. In trading, we must be prepared for such moments, which occur about every five to ten years. I was ready just enough to capitalize and begin snowballing my accounts.

Figure 1: SLGG excecution chart

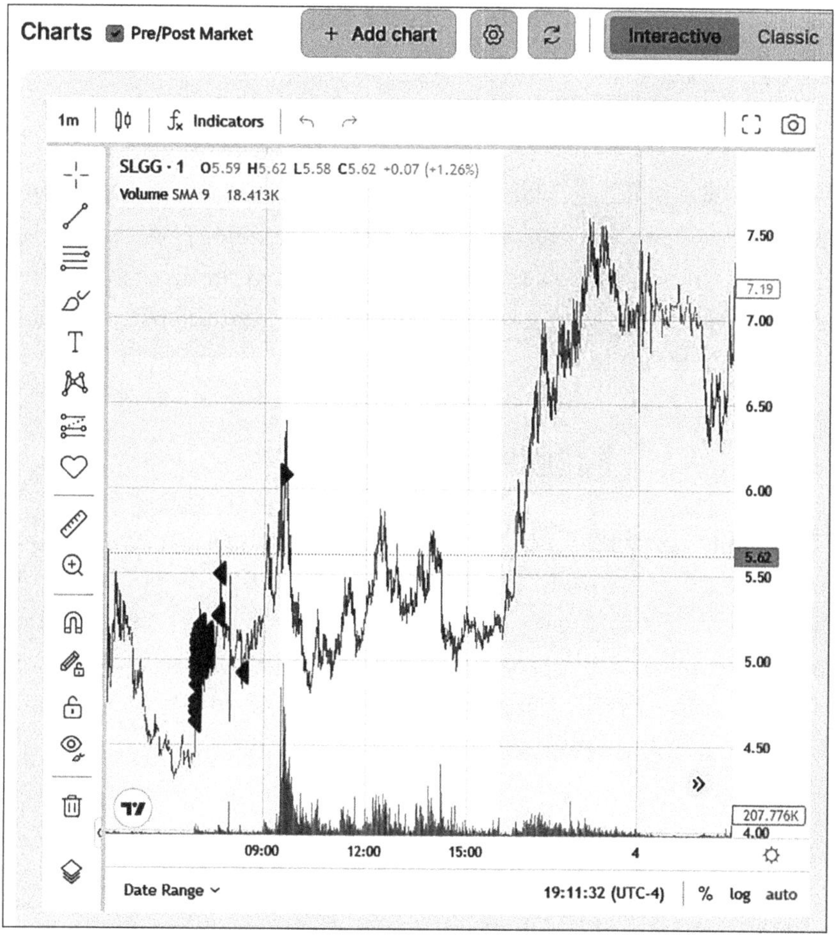

Source: *TraderVue* trading journal.

LESSONS LEARNED

DISCIPLINE IN A FRENZIED MARKET

The meme stock phenomenon of 2021 served as a cautionary tale against herd mentality and emotional trading. Despite initial losses, the ability to recover and grow highlighted the importance of sticking to a disciplined approach. Avoiding the allure of quick gains and maintaining a strategic perspective were key to long-term success.

THE SIGNIFICANCE OF MISTAKES

Mistakes are building blocks for success. Take each mistake as an indicator of how you can improve your methodology in the future and learn from it. Make a mental note and journal the error for future reference. In doing so, you will be able to recognize the patterns that emerge in later trades.

HARDSHIP IS TRANSITORY

Navigating personal challenges—from sleeping in my office to showering on Skid Row—underscored the importance of determination and focus. These hardships were temporary, serving as a backdrop to my ultimate goal of mastering the art and science of trading and drawing inspiration from market wizards who had achieved success through years of perseverance.

TIPS AND TRICKS

- **Adapt to market conditions**: Avoid swing trading in volatile markets, especially in sectors like biotech, during hype-driven periods.
- **Focus on intraday trading**: This maintains flexibility and agility, reducing exposure to overnight risks.
- **Understand market inefficiencies**: Premarket trading (4 a.m. to 7 a.m. EST) often presents opportunities due to low liquidity and weaker competition. Capitalize on these early inefficiencies.

- **Exploit uncertainty**: During periods of uncertainty, such as a pandemic, exploit inefficiencies created by irrational market behavior. Focus on sectors prone to speculation, but ensure your approach is grounded in sound research and analysis.
- **Manage risk effectively**: Always trade defensively, especially after significant losses, to prevent emotional decision-making. Remember that the market can remain irrational longer than you can remain solvent—be disciplined and manage your exposure wisely.
- **Avoid the herd mentality**: Be wary of hype-driven stocks, including those promoted by social media influencers or newsletters that can drive market sentiment. Stick to a well-defined strategy and avoid chasing trends fueled by speculation or FOMO.
- **Leverage educational resources**: Study the techniques of experienced traders and use reliable educational content to refine your skills. Tools like Japanese candlestick charting provide valuable insights for informed decision-making.
- **Embrace resilience**: Accept losses as part of the learning process and use them to adapt and improve. Maintain a positive outlook, understanding that setbacks are temporary and growth is a long-term endeavor.
- **Adopt a long-term vision**: Visualize your goals and use them as a driving force to stay committed to your path. Regularly reassess your strategies and progress to ensure alignment with your aspirations.

Chapter 3

NEW KID ON THE BLOCK

IN THIS CHAPTER, I discuss my year-long stay at a trading office in Puerto Rico, where I expanded my network with expert traders and took my discipline to a new level. My goal was twofold: first, I wanted to add value and give a voice to the short sellers of the world by providing them with a platform to engage in meaningful discourse. Second, I aimed to conduct interviews with successful traders, authors, industry insiders and financiers, and thus expand my network. I thereby began to build my identity in the short-selling niche. In doing so, I sought to demystify the true nature of short selling. The concept of 'the bear' (i.e., the short seller) generally tends to have negative connotations when it is not explained in context. My podcast was brand new at the time and could have engendered uncertainty about my intent—and about the nature of short selling. Therefore, I named my podcast *The Friendly Bear* to mitigate possible fears or misconceptions. The podcast afforded me access to knowledge that I could not acquire on my own—it was my window to the world.

REBUILDING BRIDGES

The loss of my SLGG investment was a pivotal moment which compelled me to reevaluate my path. I recalled the countless hours I had spent studying trading videos filmed in Puerto Rico and longing for a community of like-minded individuals—experts who could help me deepen my understanding and refine my skills. Determined to turn aspiration into action, I decided to visit the island in February 2021 with the goal of exploring trading opportunities and visiting one specific trading office that had caught my attention.

That journey led me to Seth's trading office, which I had first discovered on YouTube while watching from my desk in my shared office in downtown LA.

After applying for a position and undergoing a thorough interview process, I was fortunate to be offered a one-year contract. Seth welcomed me on board and my dream began to materialize.

Before moving to Puerto Rico, I returned to Los Angeles to settle my affairs. On the way, I made an important stop in Miami to reconnect with my parents after a long, self-imposed absence. That visit was unexpectedly profound—a chance to heal rifts that had quietly grown over the years. My mother greeted me with open arms. She had been there for me during the most trying time in my life (the brain surgery in my 20s). In addition, as an educator, she understood my need to excel. Born in Cuba, my mother was just two years old when her family fled Fidel Castro's rebels, who had looted and destroyed a family farm. After her grandfather was killed defending their property, the family escaped to Miami with nothing but a single bag of belongings, disguised as tourists so as not to raise suspicion. Branded traitors by the Castro regime, they never returned to Cuba. Despite these hardships, my grandparents instilled in their daughters an unshakable respect for education. That legacy shaped my mother's belief in perseverance and ambition.

On the other hand, my father—ever the pragmatist—posed familiar questions: "When are you going back to architecture? Why did you leave Miami?" I couldn't help but smile, appreciating his perspective even if it clashed with my own. Having emigrated from Iran and built a successful career as a mechanical engineer, my father had lived the American Dream, providing for our family through his steadfast commitment to a traditional 9-to-5 routine. To him, my unconventional path—leaving architecture and diving into the world of trading—was perplexing, even unfathomable.

I wished I could have explained the complexities of trading, the discipline it required, and the immense fulfillment I derived from it. I knew that, had he understood the depth of my passion and the potential for success, he would have supported me wholeheartedly.

THE LAW OF ATTRACTION AT WORK

One trait I inherited from both of my parents is the drive to keep pursuing my goals despite the odds. Being in Puerto Rico was a huge part of the aspirational vision I had conjured for my life—it was everything I had imagined. I was in my element, soaking up the atmosphere, socializing with new friends, playing softball, drinking coffee, and immersing myself in trading. I still paid a nominal rent on my small office while I stayed in a hostel for $20 a night. Just because I was a six-figure trader didn't mean I had to spend like one. More than anything, I wanted to add value to Seth's trading office, grateful to be in the presence of expert traders. So, I decided to start a podcast. I set up my microphone and RSS feed and interviewed my new, highly skilled friends, encouraging them to share their stories. The exchanges were fun, exhilarating, and informative; and as we developed a rapport, I furthered my education and network.

ESTABLISHING A TRADER'S IDENTITY

In March 2021, I started using a computer optimized for trading, with four vertical monitors, for the first time—a vast improvement on my tablet, eternal screen, monitor, and keyboard. New software also accelerated my knowledge. Inspired by these technological advancements, I resolved to renovate my office back in LA to include state-of-the-art equipment (e.g., a high-tech computer and ergonomic chair) to facilitate my trading. I traveled back and forth from Puerto Rico to LA every four to six weeks, seizing every opportunity to learn from those around me, who served as invaluable resources.

Trading had become a way of life. I lived and breathed the discipline. While my colleagues basked in the nourishing sun in the happiest place on earth, I sat at my desk from 3 a.m. to 8 p.m., relying on vitamin D3—my sunshine in a bottle. The air-conditioning hummed relentlessly, driving up the energy bill as I worked into the night.

As engaging as the camaraderie was, egos sometimes got in the way. Whenever I asked questions that evinced my 'newbie' status, the other more seasoned traders would often ignore me. I also felt 'low on the totem pole' whenever I asked Seth to be a guest on my podcast. He refused outright and was singularly unimpressed. I never knew why. I guess he just wanted me to gain traction before I had the honor of interviewing him. But I cannot lie: his dismissiveness bothered me. On one occasion, he took me aside after the market closed and told me, in no uncertain terms, "Listen, we're trying to concentrate here, and the podcast is creating too much noise."

"I created the podcast to interview traders—just like the interviews in the market wizard books—and I aspire to become a market wizard," I explained. Looking Seth straight in the eye, my voice resonating with conviction, I affirmed, "I'm never going to stop."

"Okay, Mr. Market Wizard. Just do the podcast in the conference room, not on the trading floor."

A combination of tenacity and audacity opens doors to success. I remember that conversation with Seth as if it were yesterday, and how I felt inside at the time. I was daunted but not defeated—it was a challenge that drove me.

Eventually, I went from being a new kid on the block to a respected member of the team, as I drew in other traders, mentioning the office on my podcast, infusing value and a strong work ethic in all my efforts.

Becoming part of that community in Puerto Rico was a dream fulfilled. Still, Seth never once deigned to come on *The Friendly Bear*, ignoring my requests while appearing on other podcasts at his desk right in front of me. I interpreted this behavior as a personal snub, but it only spurred me to believe in myself even more and continue moving forward. Ultimately, I was grateful to him for allowing me to join this community of illustrious traders and I never lost sight of the enduring value of that experience.

Later, I met Steve, a hedge fund analyst and trader who became a close friend and mentor. He graduated from college in California with a degree in finance. Subsequently, he worked on Wall Street for many years as a chartered financial analyst (CFA). In the early 2000s, he played online poker and gained a profit of about $500,000, which he used to get started in trading. Unfortunately, he lost most of his winnings within a few years. Eventually, he became frustrated with his job as a CFA and started his own short report research firm—a decision informed by his experience on Wall Street and keen understanding of short selling. The main thrust of his approach to the market was understanding the players on the other side and knowing who his opponents were—whether dubious actors, hedge funds, or ordinary individuals. That was one of the salient lessons he taught me.

Steve would sell information and findings to other short report outlets and other big players while also learning to trade. He embodied everything I aspired to be, exposing dubious practices through incisive short reports, thinking critically and analytically, and fearlessly calling out deception. His example inspired me to push past my limits, delve into case studies, and draft my own short reports, drawing on the research-driven approach I had honed as an architecture student. I developed watchlists and provided in-depth analyses that added value to our shared trading experiences. In addition, *The Friendly Bear* gave me the credibility I craved, serving as a refreshing change from the confines of my LA office.

LESSONS LEARNED

ADAPTABILITY AND GROUNDEDNESS

Staying flexible and emotionally grounded—whether with family, peers, or yourself—and finding peace in all spheres of life demonstrate your commitment to cherished goals. If any part of your life is in disarray, that disruption will invariably impact your trading. Embrace change while honoring the equilibrium that keeps you grounded, like connections with family and friends.

FIND MEANING IN THE STRUGGLES

The legacies of those who came before and lived a life of purpose provide impetus to find deeper meaning in your endeavors, as you align personal aspirations with innate values.

TENACITY AND AUDACITY OPEN DOORS TO SUCCESS

Unwavering commitment, even in the face of challenges or dismissiveness, underscores the value of persistence. The mantra 'I'm never going to stop' exemplifies how determination can turn adversity into fuel for achievement.

COMMUNITY FOSTERS GROWTH

Immersion in a like-minded, skilled community presents opportunities for learning and personal development. Despite early feelings of inadequacy, the collaborative environment I found in Puerto Rico ultimately provided invaluable lessons and connections for me. I needed to learn, and I always wanted to give back. *The Friendly Bear* podcast brought attention to Seth's office and served as a forum for conceptualization and learning. The shared experience is vital to collective education and empowerment.

DISCIPLINE BREEDS EXCELLENCE

Long hours, study sessions, and journaling reflect how discipline and focused effort are integral to mastering any craft—particularly one as complex as trading.

TIPS AND TRICKS

- **Seek out opportunities to learn**: Dive into environments that challenge and advance your skills and knowledge, whether through professional communities, mentorships, or self-driven projects like podcasts.
- **Balance passion with pragmatism**: Pursue your goals fervently but maintain practical habits such as managing expenses (e.g., living frugally despite financial success) to ensure sustainability.
- **Leverage technology**: Use advanced tools, such as optimized trading setups, to enhance your efficiency and effectiveness in your field.
- **Turn rejection into motivation**: Use dismissive feedback or criticism as a catalyst to improve. A steadfast mindset helps transform perceived obstacles into opportunities for growth.
- **Be persistent but respectful**: Strive to make your voice heard while respecting the boundaries and needs of those around you. The compromise to move my podcast recording to the conference room exemplifies this balance.

- **Network strategically**: Forge meaningful connections with people who inspire you. Building relationships with accomplished individuals can open doors and expand your perspective.
- **Document your journey**: Keep detailed records—whether through journaling, podcasts, or case studies—to reflect on your growth, refine your strategies, and build credibility.
- **Think critically and analyze deeply**: Develop a sharp analytical mindset, as demonstrated through detailed short reports and stock analyses. Critical thinking is invaluable for informed decision-making.
- **Celebrate small wins**: Acknowledge incremental progress and contributions—like drawing attention to Seth's office through my podcast—to maintain motivation and momentum.

Chapter 4

ADVENTURES IN BUCARAMANGA—UNMASKING A BLATANT PUMP AND DUMP

IN THIS CHAPTER, I chronicle my adventure in Bucaramanga, Colombia, where I uncovered a pump-and-dump scheme for my friend Steve's research firm. I was still residing and trading in Puerto Rico at the time. The journey seemed impossible, as the site I sought to investigate—purportedly a marijuana cultivation facility—was located in a remote, mountainous area, accessed via muddy trails and with no infrastructure. Claiming to be an architect, I armed myself with high-tech equipment to record and document my findings. I narrowly escaped with my life and learned many valuable lessons about what to look for in unveiling blatant pump-and-dump schemes.

SIGNS OF A CLASSIC PUMP AND DUMP

As I studied, read, traded, journaled, and surfed the internet, I noticed one company trading out of Bucaramanga, Colombia. Flora Growth Corp. (FLGC) had shady underwriters who had a history of stock dumps after 180 days with previous runups for little to no reason just before the shares unlocked. Underwriters are often the orchestrators of manipulation, calling the shots so insiders or shareholders can exit for profit. Theoretically, low-tier underwriters, whose reputations precede them, collude with insiders, who somehow help them with their manipulation schemes.

FLGC appeared to be a classic pump-and-dump operation, rapidly rising from $1 to $7, then to $9. The company claimed to operate a 246-acre marijuana cultivation facility, claiming *ad absurdum* that it could export marijuana worldwide at $0.06 per gram and that the total export market for cannabis would reach over $1.7 billion by 2030. The company made itself out to be utopian in its YouTube videos and social media posts—a too-good-to-be-true display of legitimacy. I was not convinced in the least.

Promotional text messages contained fine-print disclaimers revealing paid compensation for the promotion, further confirming my suspicions. "Let's do a short report on this company," I declared to Steve. "This will show them I'm serious and I'm not turning back," I told myself. I mustered all my mental resources, readying myself for a new adventure—little anticipating that I would soon need the skills of an escape artist.

UNVEILING A PUMP AND DUMP

Diving ever deeper into my crusader's role as a trader, I told Steve that I planned go to Bucaramanga to expose FLGC. The setup was perfect: my fluent Spanish and proclivity for research would be the perfect cover. Also, I would pose as an architect. No one would suspect me—or so I thought.

"Do you really want go to the mountains of Colombia, in the middle of nowhere?" Steve asked in disbelief.

"Yes—we need proof to debunk misconceptions about the company's legitimacy. The documentation will say it all," I replied intrepidly, prepared to take videos and record every move I made to achieve this.

Embarking on this venture, I thought back to my days as an architecture student, when professors encouraged us to visit and scope out a site and assess the landscape before conducting a site analysis. In this case, I sensed the journey would be a watershed moment in my new career—especially when I saw the company's co-founder and director in an old photograph (perhaps from the 1990s) with the Wolf of Wall Street, Jordan Belfort, back in his heyday. That photograph was a huge red flag: nefarious actors invariably seek out like-minded individuals. I all but had the story in the bag—I just needed a plan and a strategy to expose FLGC's suspect activity. I realized that when people invest in dubious stocks, they become defensive about the risk of losing their investment, scrambling to justify their actions despite appearances. For my report to be effective and credible, therefore, I needed irrefutable incriminating evidence.

"I will recall this story when I'm 80 years old—a tale I will perhaps tell my grandchildren," I told myself. "The timing is right and writing a well-received short report as an unknown will expand and solidify my reputation in the trading community. I'm athletic, at the height of my physical prowess, able to scale mountains."

But something was very wrong. By all appearances, the remote region of Bucaramanga in which FLGC was located was nonexistent—undetectable on any map. I scoured the internet and eventually found an obscure place near a body of water. Then, when I studied one particular photograph, I spotted the words "Finca Cantalavieja" written on the corner of a tiny wooden plaque mounted on a stick-like structure. In Spanish, the name means 'Farm of the Old Lady Who Sings.' If the scenario were not questionable, it would have been farcical.

Throwing caution to the wind, I seized my chance to explore the location and reveal the truth about FLGC, despite the obvious risks involved: the region's obscurity, the company's dubious legitimacy, and the probability of placing myself in danger by visiting the site while posing as an architect from Miami. However, the name of the game in trading is the risk/reward ratio. You can't enter into a trade without assessing the odds involved in both, and naturally, the reward must outweigh the risk. I perceived this to be true in this case and felt confident that I could uncover the questionable operation and subsequently earn the reputation of a credible, respected trader.

As FLGC was publicly listed on Nasdaq, I had the right to embark on such an expedition. So, I planned an unannounced visit and accumulated as much intel as possible through a phone conversation with a representative at the company's office in Canada. Equipped with a $100 pen camera I had purchased at a spy store in the largest mall in Puerto Rico—the only place I could find the item (Amazon takes weeks to deliver to the island)—I planned to stealthily record the entire exchange. I also purchased a polo shirt with a pocket where I could store the recording device. Meticulousness was of the essence.

Bags packed, I flew from Puerto Rico to Panama, then on to Colombia with my false exit ticket—another burning-the-boats scenario. I planned to purchase my return ticket only once I had completed my mission: I was determined not to return until I had discovered and assessed the company's status. In my mind, there was no doubt that it was a questionable operation, but I tasked myself with gathering incontrovertible proof that would prevent new investors from being duped.

I landed in Colombia on a Saturday at sunset. At around 8 p.m., I arrived in Bucaramanga in pitch darkness, having prearranged with my hostel for a pickup at the airport. Along came my affable guide on a motorcycle, who had to ride to the top of a steep mountain where the airport was located. Once we had reached our destination, I turned to him and explained that I had to go to the site in the morning (without explaining the purpose of my visit), specifying the destination and coordinates.

The next day, my bewildered guide—who was used to assisting tourists who wanted to go parasailing—looked at me with a confused expression. As we traveled through the mountainous, muddy terrain on our rented motorcycles, he intermittently asked, "Where in the world are we going? You don't want to go parasailing? It's Sunday and the sky is clear." I shook my head, steadfast in my resolve.

TELLTALE SIGNS OF A DUBIOUS COMPANY

The journey to the site was long and challenging. When we got closer, I approached locals for directions, asking "*Donde puedo encontrar Finca Cantavieja? Soy arquitecto de Miami*" ("Where can I find Finca Cantalavieja? I'm an architect from Miami").

People stared at me as though I was from Mars and pointed randomly. No one had ever before inquired about Finca Cantalavieja. The entire area—covered with dirt roads and mud, with no electricity or Wi-Fi—felt like another planet. Nevertheless, I knew the 'farm' had to exist *somewhere*. After three hours, we arrived at a gate displaying a makeshift sign featuring the company's name.

I was nervous, shaking inside, but determined to maintain my composure. My companion, the parasailing hostel employee, looked more confused than ever as security officers in camouflage gear (read: gangsters) looked at each other and then at me with heightened scrutiny and suspicion. My guide, however, was a good soul and his casual, unsuspecting demeanor helped to validate my façade.

All the while, I was thinking, "I could just vanish. I'm on the final frontier of Planet Earth. What if these guys find out I'm not who I say I am?" As my mind spiraled, I announced myself and turned on my phone and pen camera without detection. "I'm here to see Javier. The Canadian office told me to come here," I said decisively. (Javier was a low-level executive of FLGC on the ground in Colombia.)

DEFLECTION

The security guards on site—sketchy, undernourished, and covered in tattoos—had the capacity to kidnap me at any moment. They proceeded to open a gate and ushered me into a shed, calling their boss, Javier, over Wi-Fi. (Although there was no Wi-Fi in the surrounding area, the shed had its own signal.) He and other staff were away, given it was a Sunday. Everyone was confused and caught off guard. They did not know I was an investor.

"Come back for a tour in three days with a government I.D.," said one. My pen camera recorded the entire exchange.

Under the circumstances, I could not argue, but the idea of traveling three hours back along that interminable barren, muddy path was unthinkable. I suspected my guide might faint at any minute. "We have to come back?! I'd much prefer to go parasailing," his almost imploring expression seemed to say.

There was not a marijuana plant in sight—just empty space, no infrastructure, and some very scary-looking guys. All the while, I recorded and took photos without suspicion while feigning a cool exterior, hoping to document every inch of the environment and every syllable of our conversation.

THE NEED FOR 'DAMNING EVIDENCE'

From the outset, I sent all my materials to Steve—the images of the front gate, the voice recording of me in the shed, and photos and videos of the dirt roads. On reviewing my report, Steve realized that no vehicles could use these trails except motorcycles—and even they couldn't travel all the way up to the farm because the terrain was too steep, muddy, and dangerous. There was no choice but to hike the last half mile up to the entrance of the cultivation facility. The locals were used to living in such inhospitable conditions in this cartel-controlled environment. He replied, "There's no infrastructure!" This was a telltale sign of chicanery on the part of FLGC, and I had to witness it for myself, having no knowledge of such conditions beforehand.

A word to the wise

Damning evidence is crucial in exposing a pump and dump: the goal is to present such compelling proof that even committed shareholders will recognize the situation and choose to sell. This can trigger a wave of selling, as both short sellers and investors offload their positions, accelerating the stock's decline.

Exhausted, but not about to surrender, I told myself that my current predicament paled in comparison to doing my first push-up after brain surgery. On arrival back at the hostel, my guide and I discovered that our motorcycles' engines had become clogged up with mud and had malfunctioned—a narrow escape, since the bikes could have broken down at any point on the return journey, leaving us stranded in no man's land.

I believed the company took my allegations with a pinch of salt—or worse. Still, even if they wrote me off as a resentful short seller on a revenge mission of some kind, they could not ignore the fact that there was no infrastructure in this obscure region. What people thought of me was irrelevant; but they couldn't ignore reality. That was the checkmate.

Meanwhile, FLGC's stock was at an all-time high and continued to climb, followed by a massive drop. This indicated that the shares had been unlocked fully and were now being actively dumped. A waterfall of short selling—by the bag-holders (those who continue holding an investment after its price has crashed and are stuck with an asset of little value with little to no chance of recovery), the manipulators, and later the short sellers—ensued, causing a constant flow of selling pressure, a result of the increased supply due to the dumping of shares.

A word to the wise

Lockup expiration periods of initial public offerings

Small-cap stocks often show a significant rise in price close to the expiry of their lockup period. This creates a strong thesis for short selling at the right time. An effective strategy involves examining SEC filings to determine when lockup periods expire and evaluating the reputations of the investment banks and underwriters that oversaw the initial public offering (IPO).

Lockup periods mostly range from 90 to 180 days and can sometimes extend to 365 days. As stocks often experience price runups around these expiration dates, I look to initiate short positions when these deadlines approach.

For example, I visited the facilities of FLGC right at its lockup expiry. I ventured to Bucaramanga two days after its estimated expiration—my investigation was extremely time sensitive and the stock's decline (dump) was imminent. Following this date, insiders' shares were unlocked and the company released a headline that sparked excitement, generating a surge in volume and liquidity. Tactics such as these can serve as a smokescreen, enabling insiders to take advantage of temporarily elevated prices and use the incoming demand as liquidity to dump their shares after the lockup expiration date. Share dilution follows, leading to a price decline. This is a pattern with borderline dubious companies.

When a company is fresh off an IPO, it's safe to assume that 180 days from the IPO date, there will be a lockup expiration. Insiders' shares unlock and they can cash in (i.e., sell their shares for a profit). That adds extreme dilution to the stock, depending on how toxic the company is. In the case of FLGC, the underwriter was a shady financier, so dumping was a foregone conclusion.

Note: There are tiers of underwriters. There is a very high probability that low-tier underwriters will start dumping the day after the stocks unlock. This is one of the characteristics of small-cap companies—predatory financiers that dilute the stocks.

To determine whether a lockup period of 90 days, 180 days, or one year applies, search the SEC filing with Dilution Tracker by accessing the 'Filings' tab and searching through '10-Qs" or "10-Ks.' Next, click CTRL > F and type 'LOCKUP' (one word), 'LOCK-UP' (hyphenated) or 'LOCK UP' (as two words). The objective is to determine which variation produces the desired result. (Note: The company will have attempted to hide this information in the filings.) Then, cross-reference the findings against AskEdgar, using its AI software to conduct a deep dive into who owns the shares. The reputations of the IPO's managing bank and underwriter are also significant: reputable institutions have higher institutional ownership, suggesting the company has been vetted. In contrast, disreputable banks and underwriters (as seen in the case of FLGC) often manage IPOs for companies with minimal or no institutional backing—an indicator of deceptive practices.

THE ENCOUNTER

My guide and I had to wait three days for our motorcycles to be repaired. During this time, I went to visit the company's auditors in the city, as listed in the filings I had unearthed from my extensive research before my journey. But I found absolutely nothing at the address—the place was a dry-cleaning storefront. The deception was as clear as day. This was surely further blatant, unequivocal 'damning evidence.' I knew that I had to return to the site, but the mere thought of taking that journey again more than daunted my guide. "Do we really have to go back to Finca Cantalavieja? There's nothing there. Are you sure you don't want to go parasailing?"

Again, I declined. "James Bond, on a mission, does not go parasailing," I insisted. "I have a purpose and I'm going to prove my theory."

By the time the bikes were fixed it was Wednesday, and I knew more people would be at the site. This time, I documented every inch of our journey meticulously. Returning was tough, but we made it and again showed up unannounced. The guards had not anticipated that we would come back, given the difficult terrain. When they spotted us, they barred our entry at the gate. "This is a publicly traded company on Nasdaq—I must enter," I asserted, trying to contain my anxiety and fatigue. "Javier told me to return with my I.D. and here I am. I flew in from Miami to be here, and it's imperative that I see Javier. I'm not leaving until I do." I was prepared to go the distance and make a third trip to the *finca* if I had to. If the guards denied me entry, I intended to use that in my report as evidence that a Nasdaq-listed company had refused to allow an investigator visit the site.

However, just then, Javier himself emerged from the shed near the gate, about 200 feet from where I was standing. A master of manipulation, Javier styled himself as though he were some kind of luminary. His florid shirt, with its pleated neck collar, was hardly befitting this bleak location in the middle of nowhere. The incongruity between his appearance and his surroundings was stark and reinforced my suspicions that the operation was not above board.

"I'm not leaving," I repeated.

A brief stand-off ensued, and my guide's confusion escalated. Javier was visibly irate, and he raised his voice: "I'm not taking you on a tour. You cannot be here."

In fluent Spanish, I replied, "Yes, I can. You told me I could come back in three days and here I am. I spoke to your head office in Canada and…"

Before I could complete my sentence, Javier called to one of the security guards: "Eh, hombre! Look at this guy's shirt! I can see a recording device in his pocket!" Darting his eyes in my direction, he made clear his suspicions: "You're not an investor!"

Just then, Javier spotted my pen camera. "What's that hole on the top of your pen?" he asked, with the expression of an angry grizzly bear. In a sweeping gesture, he tried to grab it. Next, he lunged for my phone.

My cover was blown. After a minor scuffle (during which I managed to retrieve the pen camera and avert the loss of my phone), Javier turned, placed his hands on his waist and looked pointedly at the guards. They looked at him, then at me, as a charged silence pervaded the entire space.

My mind was racing: "This is it. They want me to disappear, and they are going to kidnap me and make sure that happens. These so-called 'security guards' are members of drug cartels and they have my fate in their hands. I'm a goner." I believed these thoughts with every fiber of my being.

A NARROW ESCAPE

My life flashed before my eyes and my heart almost leaped out of my chest as I envisioned my certain capture—and worse. Then, all at once, I turned to my guide and, almost instinctively, we both took off back to our motorcyles. Miraculously, no one followed us. All the way, I kept looking back over my shoulder, but the guards were not chasing us. No doubt they wished to remain in obscurity on that little 'farm' to save their own hides. Had they risked leaving the site and given chase, the jig would have been up because they would have revealed themselves in plain sight to be pursuing an investigator—legitimate company staff with nothing to hide would not behave in that manner.

Back on our motorcyles, we briefly took a detour down some back roads, just in case; but we were still alone. During the three-hour journey back to the hostel, my guide and I barely spoke a word to each other. What was there to say? Thankfully, my guide seemed to have little idea of the clear and present danger we were in. As for me, I was just grateful that we had both escaped in one piece.

I subsequently sought to dispel any discomfort my guide had

experienced with an extremely generous tip, for which he thanked me profusely. Before I left for the airport, I was delighted to see him and his whole family in the hostel's common area enjoying a massive Colombian pizza party, courtesy of my gratuity. I could not have been happier—he deserved every cent!

"Nobody can deny they have no roads up there—just mud paths for dirt bikes," Steve said over the phone later. "How are they going to ship marijuana to the whole world for $0.06 a gram and revolutionize the industry without roads?!"

Nothing speaks the truth like the obvious, and nothing reveals the obvious more than an in-person investigation. I had accomplished my mission and solved the puzzle.

I could not have been more relieved to plant my feet back on Puerto Rican soil. That was a narrow escape—another brush with death that I would long remember.

HOW INVESTIGATIVE PROBING CHANGED MY OUTLOOK

After my adventure in Bucaramanga, my life took a 180-degree turn thanks to the short report I authored as the lead investigator for Steve's short research firm. My experience in Colombia gave me the confidence to embody the characteristics of a successful trader and believe I had truly reached that level, shaking off the imposter syndrome that I had suffered since the start of my trading journey. In response, the luminary traders around me no longer perceived me as a novice; instead, they answered all my questions (whereas previously they had been dismissive) and were eager to hear my opinions. Others now believed in me, interacted with me freely, and acknowledged me as their equal. I had made a quantum leap forward, and my colleagues began to see me as a budding authority, no longer scoffing at or ignoring my questions.

A word to the wise

'Reverse split'

When sketchy companies dilute their stocks and sell abundantly, this often signals a pattern of incremental dilution over time, gradually eroding the stock's value to mere cents on the dollar. To remain listed on Nasdaq, these companies must meet specific criteria, including maintaining a minimum share price of $1.

To address this, they often employ a tactic known as a 'reverse split.' This maneuver does not change the overall value of the stock but alters its structure. For instance, in a one-for-ten reverse split, a company reduces its outstanding shares from 100 million to 10 million while proportionally increasing the share price. The objective is to consolidate the shares into a smaller number with higher per-share prices, ensuring compliance with Nasdaq's listing requirements.

While this process can preserve a company's listing, it often serves as a temporary fix—a sleight of hand in stock trading—masking deeper issues with the company's financial health.

'Correction'

Sir Isaac Newton's First Law of Motion offers a fitting analogy when it comes to questionable stocks and small-cap companies. Just as gravity is the unbalanced force that acts on objects in motion—slowing their ascent, bringing them to a halt, and ultimately pulling them back down—the stock market operates in a similar fashion. In financial terms, this downward movement is known as a 'correction.'

THE FATE OF FLGC

Meanwhile, FLGC's stock plummeted from $20 to $10, eventually falling below $1. This sharp decline forced the company to execute multiple reverse stock splits over time to maintain its Nasdaq listing. Currently, the stock is trading below $1 again, even after another recent reverse split. To remain on the exchange, FLGC executed a ten-for-one reverse split, temporarily raising the share price from $0.08 to $0.80 by reducing the number of outstanding shares. However, stocks trading at such low prices are challenging to short, since short sellers must post significantly more capital. Brokers typically treat stocks priced under $2.50 as if they were worth $2.50 for margin requirements, making it capital intensive to hold substantial short positions in such low-priced stocks. This makes targeting penny stocks less attractive for short sellers.

A word to the wise

Stock delistings—removal from the exchanges

If a stock trades below $0.10 for ten consecutive days, it faces imminent delisting to the OTC market under Nasdaq Listing Rule 5810(c)(3)(A)(iii). This rule mandates a 'delisting determination' for securities that fail to maintain the $0.10 threshold, irrespective of any other corrective time frame previously available to the company.

Stocks in this precarious position often experience a 'gravitational pull' effect as companies scramble to maintain a price above $0.10 to delay delisting. These efforts frequently involve issuing press releases or employing promotional tactics to generate buying interest and push the stock price over the threshold.

The minimum closing bid requirement

If a company trades for 30 consecutive business days below the $1 minimum closing bid price requirement, Nasdaq will send a deficiency notice to the company, advising it that it has been afforded a 'compliance period' of 180 calendar days to regain compliance with the applicable requirements. If it fails to do so, the company receives a deficiency notice but can often pay fees to secure extensions. For short sellers, this doesn't guarantee delisting after the 180-day window, as companies frequently manage to secure extensions or execute reverse splits to maintain their listing. The uncertainty of such scenarios often complicates short-selling strategies. To play for time, companies may also hold shareholders' meetings to consider measures like a reverse stock split. In addition, brokers impose stringent margin requirements for low-priced stocks, typically requiring at least $2.50 per share upfront. This higher capital requirement deters many short sellers from targeting penny stocks, making them less appealing to those with limited resources.

Also, it's important to note that after a reverse stock split, the float (supply) is usually too small and can easily be manipulated with very little volume (demand). I usually wait at least a few weeks to short it, until the company dilutes some shares into its freshly small post-split float.

LESSONS LEARNED

CHANNEL YOUR INNER JAMES BOND

Trusting any company's surface claims poses risks, and grandiose promises or paid promotional campaigns may signal dubious practices. Meticulous research (e.g., the CEO's background, and the intent and purpose of the company), visiting company sites, and gathering firsthand evidence will help distinguish truth from fiction.

RED FLAGS SHOULD NOT BE IGNORED

Identifying and acting on red flags in the early stages of investigation is critical in company analysis.

PREPAREDNESS AND ADAPTABILITY ARE KEY

From planning how best to navigate harsh terrain to using covert recording equipment, preparedness and adaptability in challenging situations can make the difference between the success and failure of investigative efforts. Most likely, borderline or outright dubious companies will be situated in out-of-the-way places, with storefronts as their 'headquarters.' Contact personnel will be elusive or nonexistent.

RISK MANAGEMENT IS PARAMOUNT

Just as in trading, assessing and mitigating risks in field investigations is essential. Having contingency plans in place, such as escape routes and alternative communication methods, is vital when entering potentially dangerous scenarios.

PERSISTENCE PAYS OFF

Despite the numerous obstacles I faced—including skeptical locals, inhospitable terrain, and intimidating guards—staying resolute and focused on my objective yielded the evidence needed to expose FLGC's dubious practices.

TIPS AND TRICKS

- **Master the art of self-preservation and credibility when conducting in-person investigations**: Adopt a plausible cover story that aligns with the mission and use supporting props (e.g., business cards, corporate attire) to back it up. This will help you blend into your environment and avoid suspicion.
- **Use covert technology wisely**: Invest in discreet recording devices, such as pen cameras, and practice using them beforehand to ensure smooth operation at critical moments. Investigate the laws of the states or countries in which you invest.
- **Leverage local knowledge**: Employ local guides who are familiar with the terrain and cultural nuances. They can provide insight and assistance while adding credibility to your presence.
- **Document everything**: Capture comprehensive evidence through photos, videos, and notes. Redundancy in documentation ensures that even if some data is lost or compromised, your overall findings will remain intact.
- **Stay calm under pressure**: Maintain your composure in high-stakes situations. A calm demeanor can defuse suspicions and help you navigate tense encounters with authority.
- **Plan exit strategies**: Always have a clear plan for leaving the area, including backup routes and modes of transportation. This is especially important when operating in remote or potentially dangerous locations.
- **Know the law and your rights**: Familiarize yourself with local laws and international regulations, particularly when dealing with publicly traded companies. This knowledge strengthens your position during unexpected encounters or confrontations.

- **Ensure the professionalism and integrity of short reports**: Be aware that many stock investors view short sellers negatively. Therefore, any report you produce must adhere to the highest ethical and professional standards.

Chapter 5

NXTP: MORE PUMP-AND-DUMP CHICANERY

IN THIS CHAPTER, I examine NextPlay Technologies, Inc. (NXTP). I explain recurring patterns of pump-and-dump practices and what to look for when encountering them, such as a lack of Federal Deposit Insurance Corporation (FDIC) insurance and the absence of a legitimate company location. I also explore the role of the short seller in uncovering dubious schemes.

A PUMP-AND-DUMP PROTOTYPE

FLGC was only the beginning of my journey. Then came NXTP, yet another pump and dump. A crypto bank without FDIC insurance, NXTP—now delisted from Nasdaq—was a technology-driven company focused on digital advertising, travel, and financial technology. One would expect investors to shy away from banks that lack FDIC insurance (the hallmark of illegitimacy), which guarantees government protection up to $250,000 per depositor's account in the event of a crash.

Whenever a dubious stock is delisted, that is unequivocal proof of its questionable nature. Short sellers who recognized these warning signs were correct in their assessment of the stock's condition and their predictions of its inevitable decline.

A word to the wise

Beware of the potential bubbles of the day (e.g., cryptocurrency, non-fungible tokens (NFTs), AI, quantum, electric vehicles, marijuana, meme stocks, drones), which can attract excessive demand (however temporary), consequent buying pressure, and extreme short squeezes. Equipped with awareness of a potential bubble, you can have more confidence in your trading plan. This first involves diagnosing whether a stock is bubble related. Once you have made this diagnosis, the focus shifts to alignment of your criteria and the timing of your entry.

NXTP was an obscure company with an office in San Juan, Puerto Rico. Formerly an OTC-traded stock, it was uplisted to Nasdaq on July 8, 2021, accompanied by an immediate name and ticker change. My short-selling analytics, which track stock performance patterns, identify such transitions as potential red flags. This is mainly because many OTC stocks are inherently speculative, given their minimal listing requirements and limited regulatory supervision.

On October 6, 2021, NXTP began to rise exponentially from $1.30 to a peak of almost $3.70, without any news fueling this almost 200% rise. Whenever a stock soars precipitously with no news within a short time and rises over 100%, it shows up on my radar, and I begin to investigate and run it through my process for a potential short-selling opportunity. NFTs—unique tokens that cannot be replaced by others—were all the rage at the time and beginners' luck was running rampant in the unprecedented pandemic environment. People were being rewarded for bad behavior, investing in dubious stocks as social media influencers took advantage of the climate—and the herd mentality—by touting empty shells, making outrageous claims about the capacity to amass quick wealth. Stuck at home, out of work and with a lot of free time, novice investors became hypnotized by the hyperbole. A cult environment held sway. Posts resounded with a mixture of desperation and hopes of instantaneous financial gratification. But it was all a hoax.

When I visited NXTP's registered 'office,' I uncovered the deception: the site was an abandoned kiosk, stacked with several months of uncollected mail.

NXTP was a crypto bank which was not FDIC insured. Legitimate banks are backed by the U.S. government (which covers Puerto Rico) and insure customers for up to $250,000. Crypto was surging at the time—a prime example of a bubble—and NXTP exploited this trend by creating a pseudo bank for cryptocurrency. The notion of a 'crypto bank' is inherently nonsensical, given the nature of crypto as a decentralized digital asset. The idea of a brick-and-mortar 'bank' runs counter to this concept, as physical banks are centralized under governmental regulation and control. Typically, those who endorse cryptocurrency favor retaining sovereignty over their currency without institutional interference. So, why would anyone want to place their money in an uninsured crypto bank? When NXTP began to run exponentially for several days, I recognized this as a scheme concocted to capitalize on the crypto frenzy. Once I have diagnosed a company as dubious in this way, I envision the endgame and I exercise extreme caution.

When a market bubble occurs, companies invariably seek to attach themselves to the trend, irrespective of their purported purpose. Take, as a hypothetical example, a biotech company working on a cure for a rare disorder. Suddenly, it issues a press release that it is launching a Dogecoin treasury. The stock surges amid the mania tied to crypto and the old saying 'A rising tide lifts all boats' holds true: the 'tide' is the market bubble, and the 'boats' are all those seeking to capitalize on the action. Irrespective of the company's legitimacy, the stock thus has a high probability of riding the wave, squeezing out short sellers along the way. Therefore, the identification of a market bubble is crucial, as this changes the landscape. Short sellers should reflect on the prevailing intensity of demand and the timing of their potential entry. The demand during a bubble can last for days, weeks, or months—and shorts must not fight the trend but wait patiently for the first signs of possible capitulation.

UNDERSTANDING A STOCK'S ORIGIN: IPOS VERSUS OTCS

Along with diagnosing stocks, understanding a stock's origin—its genesis—is critical. Whether a company lists on the market through an IPO, an OTC uplist, or another mechanism can materially affect its trading behavior and risk profile. Stocks are listed through various pathways and traders must understand how a given stock came into existence.

For example, stocks listed through an IPO have never previously been traded on a public exchange. As a result, IPOs have no prior chart history, meaning there are no established resistance levels above the offering price. This lack of historical resistance can contribute to extreme price movements, including potentially dangerous short squeezes. As discussed in Chapter 4, IPOs typically involve lockup periods—often six months or longer—during which insiders are restricted from selling their shares. During these lockup periods, there is a lack of supply to absorb potential short squeezes. A potential supply increase is a desirable indicator for shorting.

By contrast, OTC uplists involve companies that have already been publicly traded and have been accessible to investors for extended periods. These stocks generally do not have prolonged lockup periods and have historical price data. This prior trading history establishes inherent resistance levels, which are beneficial for short sellers. As short sellers, we must actively look for resistance levels that cause a stock to reject and begin to decline. Simultaneously, once free of lockups, insiders can sell without restriction, causing selling pressure through an increase in supply. In this case, the stock has inherent resistance levels built into its chart history and supply increases—a confluence of factors that increases conviction in short selling. Thus, you can increase your position size: knowledge, information, preparation and experience converge. Bubbles in particular afford opportunities under such circumstances.

There are various ways stocks can be listed, and traders must be able to differentiate between them. However, note that OTCs carry their own stigma on the market, as it is common knowledge that OTCs are mostly dubious. They have low-standard listing and trading requirements. (For example, they sometimes trade for under a penny a share. Hypothetically, someone hopes for a 100% gain on half a penny that goes to a penny. That individual is taking risks without forethought, which is tantamount to gambling.)

TYPICAL PUMP-AND-DUMP PATTERNS

While writing a brief report on NXTP, I began to discern recurring patterns typical of pump-and-dump schemes, marked by stock manipulation and ensuing investor frenzy:

- **Dubious CEO profiles**: Company CEOs almost invariably have dubious pasts, masked by a façade of goodwill, promises of wealth creation, and ostentatious displays of success—all style, no substance.
- **Aggressive promotions**: Paid advertisements and press releases target gullible investors, enticing them with the promise of quick riches.
- **Limited or non-existent information**: Companies often have little public information, as many are either non-existent or fronts for dubious operations.
- **Obscure locations**: Headquarters range from shell buildings and

PO boxes to far-flung offshore addresses. While NXTP's kiosk was technically easy to locate in San Juan, its remoteness likely deterred thorough scrutiny.

- **Shared obfuscation**: CEOs frequently conceal their holdings by funneling shares to associates, spouses, family members, or other entities, thereby avoiding suspicion from concentrated stock ownership. NXTP's CEO, for instance, transferred shares to both his ex-wife and his new wife to disguise his involvement.
- **Manipulated hype**: Artificial price inflation (the 'pump') entices investors while concealing the dubious activity.
- **Unsuspecting targets**: The real tragedy is the sheep—naïve investors chasing the mirage of instant wealth. They are lured by flashy symbols of success, such as gold chains and sports cars, and persuaded by empty promises of overnight fortune.

The inevitable result is a house of cards collapsing, a domino effect of financial ruin that spares no one—neither the victims nor the manipulators. The latter, acutely aware of their misdeeds, often spiral into substance abuse, masking the guilt they can neither escape nor confront.

Enter the short seller: a crusader exposing these dubious activity schemes, attempting to hold perpetrators accountable. Yet even they face a backlash from the very victims they seek to protect. "How dare you take away our dreams?" cry the disillusioned. "How can you ruin our chances at instant wealth?"

The irony is stark. The manipulators leave devastation in their wake, while the short seller—seeking justice—becomes the scapegoat; the target of misplaced outrage.

In the aftermath of the frenzy, the trading realm swarms with fans of the Joker, luring the herd to their slaughter. The images and terminology are unpleasant, but the metaphor rings true. Then, just as darkness looms, the Bat signal surges to life. A piercing beam of light cuts through the gloom and the short seller answers the call to action, halting the perpetuation of destruction. That was my idealistic vision—and I had only just begun.

LESSONS LEARNED

CONDUCT THOROUGH DUE DILIGENCE

Conduct due diligence through incisive research and journaling; do not just proceed blindly to short stocks that display the typical patterns of pump-and-dumps.

TIME YOUR ENTRIES

Timing your entries is essential, as true pump-and-dump manipulators are in control. If you are too early on the runup, you can get caught in an enormous short squeeze. Therefore, it is crucial to enter defensively until the price action reveals the back side of the runup. The beginning of the end usually starts with a crack in the daily chart (known as the 'first red day' (FRD), discussed in Chapter 10).

DON'T BE SWAYED BY MEDIA HYPE

Paid pump promotions and lures have no substance and signal stock manipulation—every time. Do not fall prey to conformism.

COMPANY LOCATION AND REPUTATION ARE KEY INDICATORS OF AUTHENTICITY

Pay attention to the location of the company's headquarters and other public information about it. Search carefully to determine whether the CEO engages in share obfuscation or funneling to other parties to divert attention from the concentration of stock ownership.

USE HOT KEYS SPARINGLY

For those new to the trading world, I don't advise using hot keys as your sole methodology if your aim is short-selling wizardry. Some beginners believe that hot keys are helpful. However, I don't use them, as I prefer to look at the bigger picture. My edge derives from intense analysis and the ability to put together all the pieces of the puzzle. I engage in high-pressure decision-making, gathering information in a high-stakes environment, using my judgment, and proceeding with discernment in every given situation. Hot keys take up too much mental space that can be utilized more efficiently by opting for a panoramic view of the circumstances. We traders can size up more effectively in this fashion—a technique that we can use equally for smaller, medium, and larger-sized plays. Moreover, this strategy is much more sustainable in the long term than reliance on quick methods of executing orders without any conceptualization. I garner various types of information and evaluate them like a hedge fund manager. That is the beauty of trading. Clicking hot keys is rote and is not conducive to short-selling wizardry, at the core of which are growth and longevity.

To survive and thrive in the trading realm, we must conduct fundamental and technical analysis and dissect news and information, using all our available mental capital, rather than simply just pressing keys on a keyboard.

TIPS AND TRICKS

- **Indications of dubious activity**: Dubious companies provide obvious clues about their operations—indicators of nefarious activity hidden in plain sight. In the case of NXTP, a crypto bank, the argument was that people don't trust banks due to hidden fees. Most people who bought NXTP did not have money to invest and bought cheap stocks, hoping for a surge. But why would anyone put money in a bank that is not FDIC insured? The investors were so influenced and caught up in the hype perpetuated by the pumpers/influencers on social media that they did not even consider whether the bank was insured.
- **The background and character of the CEO**: Research the background and character of the CEO and the individual who created the company. Sometimes, the CEO is just a puppet. In addition, multiple divorces are usually a red flag, as shares can be moved and funneled to ex-spouses through the marriage loophole.
- **Remote locations**: Companies that are remote from the U.S. mainland can be suspect, as these places are more difficult to reach—their locations act as buffers for nefarious activities. For example, although Puerto Rico is considered a U.S. territory where the SEC has jurisdiction, caution is of the essence. Puerto Rico's distance from the U.S. enables manipulators to operate with impunity.

Chapter 6
FORTRESS OF SOLITUDE

IN THIS CHAPTER, I discuss the importance of investing in myself and creating an environment conducive to continued success. I assembled a library of books I wanted to read; I upgraded my computer equipment; and I erected sophisticated wall panels in my office with the aim of improving the sound quality and my podcasting experience (which was also part of my education). The panels created a serene atmosphere and backdrop, translating into a quiet place to work. The proper environment is essential for maximized performance. This is one of the crucial factors that differentiates the successful trader from the hobbyist.

AN ENVIRONMENT CONDUCIVE TO PERSONAL GROWTH

I am on a constant quest to maximize performance. The information in this chapter is not an exercise in braggadocio. I offer this so that you can do the same in the trading game, which demands exceptionality and excellence. My environment enabled me to grow my podcast and reach out to others. The more knowledge and information I amassed, the more I directed those resources toward trading. The podcast was my window to the world.

THE PRINCIPLE OF KAIZEN

Traders who enjoy initial success must invest in themselves if they want to achieve sustainable growth. Those who seek to establish consistent success learn to resist splurging on a lavish lifestyle and instead channel their energy and resources into enhanced knowledge and self-cultivation.

The Japanese principle of *kaizen* is apt here. '*Kaizen*' means 'change for the better' and refers to incremental, continuous investment in your process, products, and work environment to make your business run like a well-oiled machine. For me, trading was not a fleeting pastime; it was a way of life. I had to be conscious of my time management because I was playing catch-up—I didn't start trading until my 30s. Having switched careers, I was behind and had to maximize my focus, time, and productivity accordingly. With a dedicated work ethic, I utilized my practices to level the playing field by putting in numerous hours of study and seeking ways to optimize my skills. I was more than okay with this approach. My methodology and time management were under my control.

As discussed in Chapter 3, during my stay in Seth's trading office, I traveled between Puerto Rico and LA every four to six weeks, slowly piecing together my office in LA in preparation for my return. The term 'piecing' here is literal, as I would order various bits of equipment and furniture components from Puerto Rico to be assembled during my trips back to LA. I did not have an apartment in LA at the time. My primary concern was establishing an office where I could trade in comfort with state-of-the-art amenities at my disposal. The preparations took about seven months to complete, and by April 2022, my 'fortress of solitude' had become a reality.

Thanks to my decision to reinvest in myself, I was poised to have a record year. In my fortress of solitude, free of the politics that can sometimes pervade office environments, I could enjoy complete focus and full control of my trading—and my destiny.

In 2022, at age 38, I realized that to enhance both my comfort and efficiency, I also needed an apartment within five minutes' walking distance of the office. This would enable me to get adequate rest while still being able to access the office immediately for trading activities and podcasts. It was time to elevate my life, both physically and emotionally. True to my nature, I envisioned a clear goal: a small, practical studio where I could shower, listen to webinars, drink coffee, take my vitamins, and trade briefly, before leaving for my office.

I organized the apartment with *kaizen* in mind, intending to use the office as my primary location for trading. The studio was a place for renewal, free from luxuries such as a television or even comfortable chairs that potentially could distract me from pursuing my trading goals, refining my strategies, meticulously journaling trades, analyzing data, and so on. After the trading day ends, every trader has a lot to do. The real work has just begun. Those who attend to this distinguish themselves from the rest and are the most successful.

A month before the move in September 2022, I ordered a Smart Bed®—the pinnacle of sleep technology—to ensure maximum comfort: I required the quality rest of a world-class athlete for optimal trading. Then, I set off on a cross-cultural adventure to Argentina, strategically timing the bed's arrival for my move-in date following my return.

Stripped of unnecessary clutter, containing only the essentials, my minimalist studio reflected the aesthetic I needed for maximum focus. It featured a standing desk; a portable yet powerful supercomputer laptop (an ASUS ROG Flow Z13 Intel Core i9—the smallest and most advanced laptop-tablet hybrid available to date); a standup pullup bar rig that served as the room's centerpiece; and, of course, my exceptional bed. This carefully curated space, designed for rest and rejuvenation, became my personal launchpad to my office across the street.

TRADING: A REFLECTION OF ONE'S SOUL AND VISION

Now that I was making consistent profits, I could focus on my performance level and implement the knowledge that I had worked so hard to amass. The purchases I made were not lavish acquisitions, but tools for optimizing my trading environment and performance. There were some perks to upgrading my environment. My office offered a sweeping panoramic view of Los Angeles from the U.S. Bank Tower. On clear days, the Hollywood sign was visible, illuminated by the sun. It was here that I pursued my lifelong quest—not solely for material acquisition (although a desire for financial freedom was the initial catalyst), but for knowledge, education, and personal excellence—a place where I could draw on my inner strength and reflect. I manifested this vision of my private space by investing in it, understanding that, just as trading is a reflection of the self, the space where one trades reflects the soul and vision of the trader.

To maintain my focus, I sometimes slept on the floor as a poignant reminder of my early days and how far I had come, compelling myself to be awake for premarket trades at 1 a.m. PST. The office was small but practical and efficient, accented by my personal preferences and requirements for speed and accuracy, creating an environment that was conducive to trading. Everything in the office was seamlessly Bluetooth-enabled. I invested in a cutting-edge Alienware gaming computer, complete with optimized liquid cooling, and paired it with a specialized trading keyboard and an ergonomic mouse. A supportive wrist guard sat alongside them. The streamlined, ultra-wide vertical monitors, mounted on customized hidden arms behind the desk, appeared to hover effortlessly—a setup designed to alleviate neck strain. For convenience, I purchased a wireless printer.

My phone rested on the wireless charger, awaiting my next call or command. Beneath the monitors sat my Echo AI device—a smart speaker developed by Amazon, ready to deliver the news, weather, and other vital updates as soon as I arrived at the office each morning. Next to it was my hub, a nexus of carefully organized wires and podcast cameras. My Bluetooth headset kept me connected, feeding real-time data from my scanners and spelling out the ticker symbols that met my precise entry criteria.

Directly on the wall to my right, near the office door, was a painting depicting the 'Burning of the Boats,' which served as a constant reminder of Hernán Cortés and the conquistadors' irreversible decision—a reflection of my own commitment.

On another wall, a depiction of the Tulip Mania boom and bust of the 17th century underscored the timeless nature of human psychology and its impact on financial volatility. Beneath my desk, a state-of-the-art air purifier quietly maintained an environment of clarity and focus. Clean air isn't just a luxury; it is essential for making sound decisions. Next to it, my bookshelf held treasured texts which I couldn't access in audio format. Two chairs adjacent to the desk were reserved for in-person podcast guests.

My podcast equipment, strategically placed to my right, allowed me to change gears effortlessly. With the flip of a switch, I could activate my camera and light dome—a setup recommended by a film-industry fan of *The Friendly Bear*, whose insights I greatly value. The camera and microphone were my conduits to the world, bringing invaluable trading knowledge into my small yet perfectly formed space.

And, of course, there was coffee—the perfect blend of energy and focus. My high-end coffeemaker stood nearby, ready to satisfy my craving for espresso whenever the need arose.

Finally, my Logitech Herman Miller special-edition chair provided unparalleled comfort, enabling me to stay seated for long periods of time. It was of the highest quality, designed by doctors and chiropractors; after installing it, I no longer experienced the back pain once caused by my rickety old chair.

Looking around me, I was struck by how everything I had envisioned for myself—the comforts of my office, my high-end tools and apps—had manifested. Everything in my inner and outer space reflected my evolution as a trader. My relatively new podcast was gaining popularity as I sought out illustrious guests—market experts and book authors. Most of my invitations were warmly received and each experience was invaluable. I was realizing my goal of being a force for change and knowledge, while simultaneously enhancing my understanding of the trading discipline and cultivating my 'master' persona.

LESSONS LEARNED

ELIMINATE DISTRACTIONS

Clear your physical space so that you can focus on trading properly. Applying the principle of *kaizen*, allow your business to run like a well-oiled machine, always making incremental improvements and ensuring your immediate environment is as organized as possible. Eliminate any clutter that could consume your mental capital and distract you. Maintain a positive, forward-looking mindset. Do not waste an ounce of energy on distractions. Put your phone on 'do not disturb.' I never allow people to interrupt my trading day, which helps me stay focused.

DISCIPLINE AND VISION AS CATALYSTS FOR TRANSFORMATION

My transition from architecture to trading compelled me to engage in incremental growth. By embracing solitude, cultivating a minimalist workspace, and investing in tools that aligned with my vision, I orchestrated a lifestyle centered on balance, achievement, and continuous self-improvement.

SELF-CARE AND PHYSICAL HEALTH

When you invest in your wellbeing, success follows, enabling you to attract what you need in life to facilitate the evolution of your 'master' persona. The more comfortable you are in your inner and outer space, the more aligned you become with your purpose.

TIPS AND TRICKS

- **Embrace improvement for focused growth**: Design your environment to align with your goals—that is, cultivate an environment that helps you achieve focused intensity in the trading niche. This involves organizing your space to make it clutter and distraction-free.
- **Invest in quality tools**: Equip yourself with high-quality tools and technologies that enhance efficiency and comfort. From top-tier computers and ergonomic chairs to carefully selected educational resources, these investments pay dividends in terms of both performance and wellbeing. However, these perks should be amassed once you become profitable. As you progress and hone your trading skills, you will be able to funnel your profits into the purchase of advanced tools, which in turn will enhance your success—another example of investing in yourself. Your advancement must proceed gradually, like building a business, keeping costs low. I didn't fully invest in my fortress of solitude until I had become a six-figure trader. The perks came later and helped push me to the next level once I had established myself in the discipline.
- **Practice incremental growth**: Achieving mastery requires consistent effort and ongoing deliberate improvements. Whether in trading strategies, workspace organization, or knowledge acquisition, incremental changes lead to long-term success.

- **Practice self-discipline**: If you don't exercise self-discipline, you open yourself up to the possibility of monumental regret that ensues from breaking rules (e.g., trading Chinese stocks or nano floats), which puts you at risk of potentially disastrous outlier losses. Such perils can be readily avoided simply by adhering to the rules. As Jim Rohn, Tony Robbins's mentor, wisely notes: "The pain of discipline weighs ounces, whereas the pain of regret weighs tons." These words apply not only to trading but to life itself. To succeed in trading, you must harness the power of self-discipline—your greatest resource over which *you* have control. Market forces are outside your control; but your ability to exercise discipline lies within you and ultimately determines the degree to which you succeed in becoming a pro trader.
- **Envision yourself as a professional trader**: If you decide to trade, you must envision yourself as a professional trader and act the part even before you attain that level of expertise. Professional traders follow their rules and cultivate routines and habits that are conducive to steady, continuous improvement (e.g., reviewing their trades and going over their charts consistently at the end of each trading day and on weekends). Tenacity and relentless resolve—which any top-level athlete possesses—are key for traders, both in their discipline and in their everyday lives. This involves enhancing and constantly refining your trading strategy through rigorous study and implementation.

Chapter 7

CHESS GAMES WITH THE BOOGEYMAN

IN THIS CHAPTER, I discuss why it's crucial to spot Chinese stock manipulation. I explain the nature and behavior of these stock patterns and the absence of strict offshore regulations. I also recount my encounter in Dubai with the protagonist of *The China Hustle*, a 2017 film which confirmed my findings pertaining to stocks coming from China. Nevertheless, despite my better judgment, I still shorted TDH Holdings Inc. (PETZ), FingerMotion, Inc. (FNGR), and TOP Financial Group Limited (TOP), resulting in significant losses. Here I reflect on the importance of learning from these mistakes.

THE SIGNIFICANCE OF THE ENDGAME

If a company is a dubious pump and dump, I can instantly foresee the endgame—the inevitable crash. *Beyond Greed and Fear,* by Canadian economist Hersh Shefrin (1999) (who was a guest on *The Friendly Bear* podcast and from whom I learned directly), offers valuable insights into the impact of behavioral psychology on stock analysis. Chart patterns are visual representations of human emotions that drive buying, selling, and the inevitable bubbles. It's important to recognize that many small-cap companies aren't necessarily nefarious; they're often just trying to survive and raise funds from their listing on the exchange. Not all stocks are questionable. But traders must approach the landscape with a measure of skepticism, as so few of the small companies in question evolve and grow.

The short seller must be armed with knowledge and timing, ready to capitalize on companies' declining stock patterns. The short seller understands that these patterns invariably ensue from manipulation. Therefore, one cannot be positive in the stock market. Instead, every move must be undertaken with wariness and caution.

When nefarious manipulators look to create a short squeeze, they most likely will examine two factors affecting short sellers:

1. the countries in which the short sellers are located; and
2. short sellers' pain thresholds, caused by overwhelming moves against them which force their exit from their positions.

It's important to recognize that there is a gray area between traditional manual wash trading and more sophisticated market manipulation. Manual wash trading involves manipulators buying and selling shares among themselves to artificially inflate a stock's price and create the illusion of strong demand. The goal is to lure unsuspecting investors into buying the stock based on this false demand. At the same time, these manipulators deliberately push prices toward levels that trigger short sellers' predefined 'maximum pain' thresholds, forcing them to exit their positions.

In many cases, overseas manipulators use predatory, algorithm-driven short-squeeze tactics. These tactics are most effective when nefarious actors can identify where short sellers are positioned. They do this by reverse-engineering executed trades from time-and-sales data and tracking short-locate inventory. By aggregating short-locate information across multiple brokerages, manipulators can effectively map out clusters of short positions and identify their vulnerability.

Once these short-seller clusters are identified, they become prime targets for manufactured short squeezes. Wash-trading schemes—often originating outside U.S. jurisdiction—are responsible for some of the most severe and damaging short squeezes. Manipulators closely monitor where short positions are concentrated and watch for signs of stress, timing their attacks to force capitulation.

The most aggressive forms of this manipulation frequently involve stocks tied to foreign markets, particularly China, where jurisdictional limits and opacity can make enforcement more difficult.

I must qualify the following remarks regarding stocks emanating from China. In no way whatsoever am I seeking to disparage Chinese culture, traditions, or people—all of which I hold in the highest regard, with deep respect, admiration, and love. As a global citizen, I embrace the richness of cross-cultural exchange: the beauty of diverse languages, arts, architecture, and ideologies. Without multiculturalism, the world would be far less vibrant and inspiring. My experience and knowledge of Chinese stocks pertain solely to traders who engage in manipulative practices. While these particular examples may be based in China, such unscrupulous behavior knows no borders. The boogeyman can be anyone, come from any culture, and play chess anywhere. It's not about race; it's about the character, psychology, and emotional makeup of the individual trader.

IDENTIFYING CHINESE STOCK MANIPULATION

Why is it crucial to spot Chinese stock manipulation? Every trader needs to establish their own set of personalized trading rules. Sometimes, this means avoiding entire categories of stocks, as long-term sustainability in the market demands such analysis, discernment, and caution. By avoiding an entire category with a greater propensity for black swan events, short sellers limit their exposure to such scenarios within that category.

I became aware of the nature of Chinese stocks from short reports and *The China Hustle*—one of my favorite documentaries, which I have watched about ten times over the years. The film follows a short report firm exposing dubious activities by companies in China. The protagonist, a Canadian Asian hedge fund analyst, travels to China only to be arrested at the airport. Most likely, the company he was investigating paid off the authorities to apprehend him because he had exposed their deceptive practices. The penalty: two years in a squalid prison. I was riveted. Little did I know at the time that our lives would eventually intersect.

DUBIOUS CHINESE STOCK PATTERNS

My podcast interviews with Chinese stock underwriters on Nasdaq and NYSE, along with conversations with leading short report firms and analysts based in Asia, confirmed the intelligence I had gathered through extensive research. As I journaled and followed short report investigations, I began to recognize the patterns. Invariably, the ticker symbols were meaningless; the company and its owner were unknown; the name lacked significance; and the company's purpose was vague at best.

During the Covid-19 era, these companies were particularly elusive, as their legitimacy couldn't be questioned—the U.S. had no jurisdiction over them, and with the world in lockdown at the time, no one was conducting investigations. Even if someone were brave enough to consider a probe (as in the documentary), this wasn't currently possible, as borders were closed to foreigners.

So, companies in China exploited the legal loopholes of the U.S. exchanges—Nasdaq and the NYSE—by forming companies through offshore entities in the Cayman Islands, the British Virgin Islands, or other Caribbean islands.

These companies also frequently complicated matters by creating intricate, layered filings, employing backdoor tactics. Due to the lack of strict offshore regulation, companies in China were able to circumvent the stringent rules and regulations to which U.S. companies are always subject.

While some naïve traders viewed these pump-and-dump schemes as quick money-makers, I knew better. Whenever I had podcast interviews with Chinese stock underwriters, I would often short the stock cautiously, little by little, and add to my position incrementally as I awaited 'the dump' over several days or weeks. Predictably, it would crash. However, every so often, the squeeze would be exponential. The stocks' movements departed from the typical U.S.-based pump-and-dump pattern that had brought me so much success as a short seller. Aristotle once said: "The more you know, the more you realize you don't know." This insight drove me to seek wisdom from those with experience in shorting Chinese stocks. Initially, I thought I was merely doing my job—identifying and exposing potentially manipulative practices.

The stocks were so opaque that I suspected some of the companies might not even exist. Adopting a cautious and methodical approach, I shorted selectively and experienced modest gains. Although skeptical, I was unwilling to close the door on potential opportunities. Renowned stock analysts, including a leading expert on Asia who frequently traveled to Hong Kong, validated my research and theories about the manipulative practices of traders in China.

FEDERAL REGULATORY SHIFTS

Before President Trump left office in 2020, the SEC and his administration imposed strict regulations on China. These had a trickle-down effect on the stock market and Chinese IPOs were paused. Companies that failed to comply faced possible delisting from the U.S. exchanges. This crackdown likely left manipulators from China wary of delisting, leading them to scale back their pump-and-dump schemes. They found themselves in a precarious position, forced to take gains quickly, making their actions more predictable.

However, when the Biden administration took office, the pauses were reversed and Chinese IPOs resumed. With that reopening, a wave of questionable listings entered the market—some producing extreme, short-lived returns of thousands of percentage points. Previously, exchanges resorted to indefinite T-12 halts when suspicious activity was identified. Now, with no way to verify the information of companies outside the U.S. jurisdiction, traders and boiler rooms in China and other remote locations (if not in China, then most likely with ties to China) were once again able to exploit unsuspecting investors, and the manipulators became more brazen and greedier than ever. Free to roam in their niche, off the radar, they ran pump-and-dump schemes that momentarily inflated these pseudo companies, many of which would subsequently crash to cents on the dollar.

A MEETING WITH THE PROTAGONIST OF *THE CHINA HUSTLE*

In 2022, a chance encounter backed up my observations of practices in China when my friend Steve connected me with a hedge fund manager who had worked with the protagonist of *The China Hustle*. The manager, in turn, introduced me to that very gentleman. We arranged to meet in a coffee shop in Dubai. I flew there to meet him and address other issues, and we spent an entire day discussing his harrowing stint in a Chinese prison for exposing one of these stocks in a short report of his. He spoke candidly, answering all my questions, and together we pored over my extensive spreadsheets cataloging the various direct and indirect manipulative practices I had been charting. He was astounded by my documentary evidence, which consisted of data that supported every single detail I had gathered over a long period of time. I also mentioned that I had conferred with prominent hedge fund activists and uncovered irrefutable proof of dubious activity. This memorable exchange confirmed my findings, which were apparent neither to short sellers nor to gullible long traders alike.

Initially, manipulators from China targeted inexperienced, vulnerable individuals whom they messaged on social media, using false profiles and assumed identities. However, as more short sellers began recognizing the liquidations, the short side became overcrowded with greater possibilities for outlier short squeezes. Short selling requires more capital to short than to buy outright. During a short squeeze, stocks can theoretically surge infinitely and then fall to zero. Therefore, the manipulators wanted to squeeze the short sellers as much as possible. Short sellers have seen these squeezes caused by stocks from China rise thousands of percentage points against them—squeezes that can lead to complete financial ruin.

Recognizing the greater profit potential on the short side, Chinese manipulators flipped the script. While gullible investors continued to fall for their manipulative practices, rather than using the traditional pump-and-dump activity of classic boiler rooms of the past, the manipulators reversed their strategy: engineering short squeezes to force short sellers out of positions violently towards the upside, using the short sellers for exit liquidity. Previously, they dumped on the longs for that purpose. But when the manipulators realized that there was more money to be made in squeezing the shorts (as the shorts had more capital), these became the prime target. By luring short sellers into believing stocks were prime shorting opportunities, they triggered massive losses by squeezing out the shorts.

THE PETZ DEBACLE

It's important to reiterate that short sellers are usually better capitalized than long traders, as we need to use margin to achieve our goals. Moreover, to short sell a significant amount, a short sell account must be considerably over the PDT rule (typically $30,000–$50,000 for the average 'small-sized' short seller). One can imagine what a 'medium' or 'large' short seller account might look like—as opposed to long traders with a Robinhood-style app or an online brokerage with only a few hundred or a few thousand in their account.

Despite my ever-increasing knowledge and caution regarding such stocks, I went against my better judgment on September 30, 2022. Believing I could defy the obvious and fully aware of the potential risks, I shorted PETZ, a company in the pet food industry. In doing so, I broke my own rule about chasing exponentially declining stocks. In this case, the stock was trading around $1.20 before it dropped to $0.89. I made a rookie mistake by chasing the stock down on negative offering news. This occurs when a publicly traded company announces that it plans to issue additional shares of stock, which often leads to a decline in the stock's price. I thought the stock would go to or below $0.89, which was my target level that I derived from the offering price. The stock capitulated to the offering price and I had a brief, unrealized profit. Then, it precipitously spiked. The stock had an outlier, massively manipulated in the after-hours squeeze to $9, since the manipulators in China most likely bought up the float. I ended up covering two days later, resulting in a $60,000 loss—an expensive lesson. It hovered around that price for weeks before finally dropping permanently.

A word to the wise

Sometimes the lessons are not worth the price—the lessons must outweigh the losses. The way to ensure this is by trading small in the early stages of learning. The game is all about surviving your learning curve. It's good to learn from the losses, but do not put yourself in a position where you might experience a black swan event that could lead to devastation and financial ruin.

Never short stocks on weakness and don't chase down offerings. I discovered various types of pitfalls to which stocks from China were more susceptible than any others. Many were in boiler rooms—most likely in remote parts of the world where traders, essentially held hostage, operated under duress. This kind of manipulation, orchestrated through mass text messages, sought to deceive unsuspecting individuals into investing in pump-and-dump schemes. Some impostors even posed as young, lovelorn girls on social media, preying on the affections of their targets with pseudo profiles. Some short sellers who infiltrated these groups revealed that in some instances, the manipulators confessed they were males—incriminating admissions that further bore out the truth. They targeted people who were particularly gregarious and sociable, establishing romantic connections to gain trust. Once a rapport was built, the pseudo personas would persuade their victims to invest in stocks from China, luring them with promises of wealth. "My uncle has a great stock tip," they would say. "If you love me, you'll invest, and we'll share the profits and run away together." But the stocks were worthless and many fell victim to the manipulators, losing fortunes.

THE HKD LURE

One example that occurred in August 2022 concerned AMTD Digital, Inc. (HKD) stock, which came through the Cayman Islands and was listed on the NYSE. Upon visiting the NYSE for the first time (by invitation only)—a highlight of my career to date—I observed the stock closely. I looked up at the board and noticed it was trending higher at an alarming rate. I already knew it was a dubious IPO before observing it at the exchange, as it had been running for a few days and was still on its precipitous rise while I was there. I also asked around at the NYSE, just to spark conversation.

"Hey! Check out HKD! Are they going to T-12 halt it? That's insane, man!" I observed.

People just chuckled and replied, "No, I don't think so. I heard some guy is high on drugs in Southeast Asia somewhere, buying it up, thinking it's the Hong Kong dollar! Haha!"

That was the prevailing joke at the prestigious NYSE. HKD IPO-ed at $7.80 and over the following nine days, it would gradually run all the way up to a peak of $2,555—for no reason at all. Everyone—brokers, market makers, professionals—just laughed it off without explaining what could be done about it. It's important to note that this event occurred on the NYSE, the most prestigious exchange on Wall Street, with a time-honored reputation for strict listing requirements. That was baffling. Subsequently, manufactured squeezes of that magnitude have not occurred on the NYSE, suggesting that the exchange has likely applied more stringent rules since.

The core foundation of my short-selling strategies is knowing and playing by the rules and using them to my advantage by implementing them according to my established practices. In the absence of rules, the entire exercise of short selling has no meaning—it's like playing chess without a queen. You don't want to play chess with the boogeyman, as you will be at an extreme disadvantage.

Sadly, one eight-figure trader, whom I'll call 'John,' wasn't so fortunate as to understand that lesson and lost $400,000 when the stock rose to unsustainable levels. Despite the emotional and physical toll, John agreed to discuss his loss on my podcast. His pain was palpable and I felt deeply empathetic—it's heartbreaking to see someone in that position. John's candor and transparency were commendable. I admired his courage and forthrightness.

Another guest who appeared on my podcast was Pedro, a Canadian YouTuber who knew of the questionable operators and enjoyed toying with them. He wasn't a trader but an astute observer of the fiasco. He told me that an individual he had spoken with in China, named 'Alina,' admitted that the manipulators were targeting long traders and would dump the stock on them. That declaration seemed to be an admission about the dubious practices at play; but a few months later, the same individual revealed short sellers to be the impostors' prime targets, as they shifted their focus from long traders. This confirmed my suspicion that they had changed tactics.

THE FNGR DISASTER

My exposure to these experiences and others should have been serious red flags; but back then, my trading approach was not as refined as it is today, and I couldn't always tell where a stock was domiciled or double and triple-check that information, as I do now with sophisticated software. When FNGR came along on October 3, 2022, barely two months after John's colossal loss, the stock seemed highly dubious; but since the company purported to have a New York office, I thought that it checked out according to my process.

I swung the trade over the weekend, flew to New York to accept the 2022 DAS Trader Award at Nasdaq, where the ceremony was held, and closed the trade when I returned to my hotel, right after ringing the bell. That trade resulted in a $100,000 loss. What a bittersweet experience! I received the honor with a mix of deep gratitude and complete devastation. When a photographer snapped my photo, no one could tell what I was thinking and feeling. I hide my emotions quite well. I was the only person who knew what had happened—until now. The photo still serves as a kind of weird testament to how I felt at that consequential moment.

Later that day, I visited the Empire State Building and Rockefeller Center's Top of the Rock (an observation deck located at the top of 30 Rockefeller Plaza, offering breathtaking views of the New York City skyline), ate a good meal, and then flew back to Los Angeles. Throughout the flight, I thought about how to rebound from my ordeal. The answer was simple: I just had to do my utmost to double-check a stock's domicile and pay attention to the insider ownership.

At the time, FNGR had an outrageous insider ownership of about 90%, which indicated control of the stock's outstanding shares. That meant the stock could easily be manipulated. "From now on, I'll trade small, get my confidence back to normal levels, and make a comeback," I thought to myself. In trading, as in life, resilience is essential; and with perseverance and strategic planning, I recovered the loss within a few months, finishing the year at my best up to that point in time.

THE ILAG LANDMINE

After regrouping for a few weeks in Los Angeles, I flew to Miami for a trading conference. I used this period to temporarily step away from my own trading and focus on my discipline. My goal was to network and discuss market trends. At that time, all eyes were on Intelligent Living Application Group Inc. (ILAG)—a Chinese manufacturer of mechanical lock sets that debuted on October 14, 2022. By not shorting ILAG, I managed to dodge a beartrap that ensnared both seasoned and novice traders. Even systematic traders, who relied on their strategies and stop-loss orders, were caught off guard. They believed they had discovered a foolproof method of risk management and could outmaneuver the market manipulators. However, traders in China bypassed the stop-loss mechanisms by controlling the supply, causing the stock to gap up when the stock unhalted after a forced volatility halt, skipping over the stop-loss triggers. (Stop losses are risk management tools to hold traders' positions and prevent losses once a stock reaches a certain price. At that point, the broker must buy or sell the security to avoid further potential loss. Stop losses are never exact; sometimes there's slippage—at certain times more than others.) As a result, many traders—particularly systematic traders who believed they had their systems figured out and in place—lost their entire accounts, some owing money to their brokers. Their data and back tests did not account for outlier scenarios such as this. In extreme circumstances, some lose everything and must declare bankruptcy.

It pained me to hear of these disasters. I commiserate with hardship and rejoice with good fortune, always mindful that none of us is immune to the fluctuations of circumstance. I was very lucky not to have gone near ILAG, as I was traveling for the weekend and wanted to be at my best for the conference in Miami and spend time with my mom (unfortunately, I could not see my dad during that visit, due to scheduling conflicts). But every pop and drop of that magnitude taught me a valuable lesson: in trading, it's important to pay heed to and learn from others' mistakes.

Upon my return to LA, I intensified my documentation of trades originating from China. ILAG reaffirmed my conviction about Chinese stocks. I began by analyzing the common denominators between stocks in China and those in jurisdictions such as the Cayman Islands, with the same underwriters repeatedly appearing in the filings. I analyzed candlestick patterns meticulously, remaining particularly vigilant whenever I detected extreme volatility or the faintest hint of dubious activity.

SHORT-SELLING ACTIVISM

Armed with my newfound knowledge and determined to prevent further disasters caused by stock manipulation by traders in China, I felt ready to raise the issue with anyone. In mid-April 2023, the perfect opportunity arose when the publicist for someone at a prominent small-cap investment bank, known for its track record of listing questionable companies on the exchanges, reached out. She praised my podcast and expressed interest in having a banker, 'Jim,' appear as a guest to discuss the Italian soccer team he owned. A quick Google search revealed that he was "head of China" at his investment bank, which had been behind the IPO of PETZ. It became clear that neither Jim nor his publicist had any understanding of the focus of my podcast or the depth of my research into questionable stock operations emanating from China and short selling generally.

Obviously, the publicist did not understand what *The Friendly Bear* meant. The designation 'Bear' clearly connotes a short seller, right?

"This guy wants me to pump the stock, assuming I'm an uninformed YouTuber/podcaster with a camera," I thought. But educating him about short sellers wasn't my goal—exposing questionable practices through activism was. So, I resolved to ask the tough questions and put him on the spot. Despite my determination, I was anxious about the interview, wondering how I could get him to reveal the truth.

Determined to devise a game plan, I began with respectful, routine questions about his background, allowing him to talk freely. He boasted about his education and connections—his wife was descended from Italian royalty. Gradually, I steered the conversation toward more pressing matters: the manipulation of traders in China, boiler rooms, pseudo identities, IPO halts, circumvention of SEC guidelines, and even *The China Hustle* documentary. As soon as I broached these topics, Jim's demeanor shifted. "I don't know anything about that," he insisted, stumbling over his words. It was clear he felt cornered.

I went on to mention TOP, a stock that deceptive investors were targeting for their next short squeeze liquidation (i.e., their use of short sellers as fuel to liquidate their supply when stock dumped at high prices, forcing the short sellers to cover their positions and sustain enormous losses). I pressed on, homing in on the core issues, while Jim attempted to deflect. He called *The China Hustle* "great entertainment," with "great actors." His discomfort grew until he abruptly changed the subject, dramatically putting on his soccer team's souvenir scarf and insisting we focus the conversation on them instead.

"The team consists of unhoused individuals and former felons playing soccer together," he declared. "It's about building friendships, not making millionaires. There's a lot of evilness and greed in sports ownership—rich people just wanting to profit."

I looked at him, thinking silently: "You're an astronomically wealthy banker who married into Italian royalty. So, what you're saying doesn't sound logical."

Finally, I thanked Jim for appearing on the podcast and we moved forward with our respective lives.

A short while later, I received a call from the *Financial Times* in London. A journalist had seen the podcast and was struck by my guest's audacity in failing to own up to his wrongdoing. Sometimes, even in the face of being called out, the artful manipulator will desperately attempt to insulate themselves from the truth and portray themselves as unwitting and innocent.

THREE STRIKES—BUT NOT OUT

Unfortunately, even with all my conviction and extensive research, I still fell prey to the dubious TOP. I had been aware of the liquidation play in China in the previous two weeks. Usually, the exponential squeeze of short sellers occurred with the manipulators' newly targeted stocks. So, I thought enough time had passed for their next pump scheme, assuming TOP was on its way out—but I was dead wrong.

On the surface, the stock fit all my criteria: the float was over $2 million; the stock was up over 40% on the day; the borrow-fee rate was under 100%; the institutional ownership was low; and I knew it was a deception. The manipulators were pumping it. I was fully aware of the company's status—that it was most likely a phantom, manipulated by boiler rooms. In other words, I knew I was trading against the boogeyman, who wasn't playing by the SEC's rules, devoid of a moral compass. In this chess game, I was playing with pawns, while the company had queens. I only knew the manipulators were targeting the stock, which would eventually collapse. I shorted the stock multiple times, scaling in at an average of around $12 a share. I covered it at $22 in the last second of the day (the stock went $10 against me); but in the after-hours, it rose to $260 a share. (In hindsight, my cover was actually favorable.) Up until that point, I'd had a $172,000 month and toward the end of this run, I was getting away with sloppy, oversized trading, which was bound to catch up with me.

Having seen the horror stories of HKD and ILAG, how did I not learn? This event confirmed, once and for all, what I had long known all too well: the manipulators were targeting short sellers everywhere—relentlessly. Just three days after my birthday, I lost $150,000. Dejected, I called the old poker adage to mind: 'If you can't spot the sucker at the table in the first hour, then you're the sucker.' That description aptly applied to the short sellers.

NEVER RISK RUIN

I also learned another vital lesson: losses make you better—but only if you don't allow them to take an emotional toll. The disaster hurt me, I cannot lie; but it gave me pause to reflect and redouble my conviction—never again would I short stocks from China. Although I had enjoyed success with many such stocks, one bad trade can potentially end a career. Never risk ruin. "I have my rules, and I must stick to them," I vowed. "That is the nature of this stock. If I stay away, I'll be fine. I will recover. I'm still alive, and I still have my trading accounts and can rebound from this, just as I did from the previous outlier loss with stocks from China. I won't have to return to Skid Row ever again."

This was my mantra as I reconstituted myself and recovered from the loss within a few months. As detractors waited for me to fail, I began a meteoric ascent.

LESSONS LEARNED

CONFIRM YOUR THESIS

Confirm your thesis about each trade and determine who or what is on the other side. When in doubt, remain small in your position and do not add to it. Timing is of the essence.

AVOID FOREIGN STOCKS WITH AGGRESSIVE MANIPULATION SCHEMES

Avoid foreign stocks, especially those with aggressive manipulation schemes—and specifically Chinese stocks or stocks with even a remote tie to China, because stock manipulators may have access to insider news ahead of time. Chinese stocks operate outside the jurisdiction of the SEC and have demonstrated a statistical tendency to squeeze short sellers more aggressively than any other stock category in recent history. The resulting volatility often renders traditional risk management strategies ineffective, leading to potentially catastrophic losses. The impact on investors can be severe, with entire careers sometimes ruined by the unpredictable nature of this category. Given these risks, avoiding Chinese stocks altogether is a prudent course of action.

DON'T BE LURED BY STOCK WEAKNESS AND OFFERINGS

Never short on weakness and don't chase down offerings. Stocks that rise too much, too fast—exhibiting overextension and perceived strength—offer both unique opportunities and inherent risks. As traders, it's crucial to identify market fluctuations and distinguish between stocks that experience rapid gains without sustainable volume and those that lack a competitive edge for effective trading. This disciplined approach—breaking down parts of the whole—keeps me grounded. When a stock declines, I avoid shorting it, recognizing that chasing it out of FOMO reflects human weakness, not the discipline required for successful trading. That's why shorting on strength is so crucial—it's the primary component of all my strategies.

CAREFULLY CHECK DOMICILE AND THE EXTENT OF INSTITUTIONAL OWNERSHIP

Don't ignore the obvious. Always double-check the stock's domicile and the percentage of insider ownership.

STOP LOSSES ARE NOT ALWAYS SECURE

Don't rely on stop-loss orders, which are susceptible to slippage. They are never exact.

ACTIVISM IS THE HALLMARK OF THE DEDICATED SHORT SELLER

If you perceive an injustice, call it out through open dialogue and diplomacy.

NEVER RISK RUIN

Losses lead to self-improvement. However, never risk ruin. Stick to your rules and your process. The lessons learned from losses must supersede the losses themselves.

TIPS AND TRICKS

- **Select stocks intelligently**: Choose stocks that are suited to your trading strategy or the types of moves you are seeking. Pay attention to your trading 'diet' and eliminate stocks you don't trade well. One mistake within these categories can end your entire career.
- **Strategic positioning is essential**: Strategic positioning is crucial to dodge pitfalls within the trade. By avoiding certain stock categories, I sometimes miss out; but that doesn't matter, because in the final analysis, my trading is sound—and so is my account.

Chapter 8

THE ARCHITECTURE OF MY PROCESS

IN THIS CHAPTER, I discuss the state-of-the-art trading software that assists in weeding out foreign stocks (particularly those emanating from China). I reflect on my *Business Insider* verification and how that affected my outlook. In addition, I present my intraday trader checklist—ten essential requirements for short selling success—along with an intraday trader questionnaire. I highlight the importance of conceptualizing trades before and after entering them, which is as crucial as chart analysis. Finally, I summarize the difference between foreign and domestic stocks.

REEVALUATING MY PROCESS

After that pivotal TOP loss, my confidence took a hit. The experience forced me to reevaluate my entire trading process—particularly my approach to foreign stocks. I realized the urgency of eliminating Chinese stocks from my trading 'diet' and the need for more careful analysis of all foreign stocks. To this end, I invested in top-of-the-line software, such as the following:

- **Trade Ideas**: This is not only a trading scanner—you can set it up with a panel that points out where a company is domiciled with text and visual images, such as flag colors. This keeps me alert to the stock's origin and ensures nothing slips through the cracks.

- **Dilution Tracker**: This displays the country name with text on top. However, it should be cross-checked for accuracy against Trade Ideas, as this software—along with Yahoo Finance—indicated that FNGR (my $100,000 loss) was a U.S. stock, when it was really from China. It is thus imperative to verify the stock's origin to avoid being blindsided. I also go through the filing section of this software to determine ownership and domicile. Even if a stock is not from China but has business dealings there (e.g., if a biotech company has labs in China), when news comes out, the Chinese have access to that information in advance and can thus manipulate the stock (even if it is a U.S.-based company) to target short sellers, who are at a major disadvantage. Sometimes, the Chinese buy up the floats, control the stock's supply, and play games, which I assiduously avoid. As the SEC does not exercise jurisdiction in China, no one can enforce rules on these companies. As my statistics, data, and precise trade journaling methods have indicated that I don't trade these stocks well, I go on high alert whenever they pop up and adjust accordingly. As a seasoned practitioner, I have developed a thesis about the odds and invariably I lose money on these stocks over the long term. Even if a company is not based in China but merely has some kinds of ties to China, or insiders with a nexus to China, I avoid it like the plague.
- **Proprietary bots**: Proprietary bots were coded into *The Friendly Bear* discord with a list of several vital criteria, one of which is the country. When the bot populates data, such as the company ticker, the ticker is hyperlinked to the company's profile page on Yahoo Finance, which displays the names of individuals on the board of the company. If these individuals (e.g., the CEO and directors) have Chinese surnames or insider ties to businesses in China, I check to determine whether the company does business there.

- **Ask Edgar**: This AI-based software allows me to ask questions on the 10Q or the 10K—for example: 'Does this company have any dealings with China?' Also, this software displays the flag of each country and allows me to triple-check information, such as where the company is domiciled. The Ask Edgar programmers are constantly updating and improving the software. However, it is important to curate information with the appropriate questions. Do not allow the software to influence your trading decisions. You must have preexisting skill and knowledge of how to review filings manually, so you know what to look for and can ask the right questions to make sound trades.

The above methodology ensures an accurate picture of my trading landscape.

BUSINESS INSIDER VERIFICATION

By 2023, I had conducted hundreds of podcast interviews, my understanding of my craft was growing by the day, and my continuously evolving trading knowledge was reflected in my performance. That same year, a journalist from *Business Insider* (now rebranded as *Insider*) contacted me to discuss my process, as I had a 90%-plus win ratio—an anomaly in the trading world. I never discussed this aspect of my work, as no one would believe me and I enjoy engaging in positive, concerted action, not braggadocio. Only a couple of friends knew of my advancements. Besides, my percentages are a by-product of how I trade; I'm fixated on the process alone. It's important to note that this is earned media, which can't be bought. Earned media outlets heard about and reached out to me, verifying my approach multiple times.

I freely opened my books and invited auditors and mathematicians to verify my results. The *Business Insider* journalist pointed out that very few traders produced their statements as I had—even with their purported high win ratios. Without verification, it was difficult to prove their claims of success, as they did not publish verifiable statements or proven results.

This auspicious opportunity was the first public recognition of my accomplishments. By this time, my imposter syndrome had evaporated; my guilt had vanished; I compared myself to no one; and, most importantly of all, I realized that my success was not a fluke. This was real: verification by one of the most reputable sources in the industry.

INTRADAY-TRADER CHECKLIST

The *Business Insider* journalist meticulously delineated my process into ten indicators.* Although the observations in that interview still apply today, I have since revised some of my strategies, as set out below. This guidance can be viewed as being akin to a pilot's preflight checklist, aimed at preventing unexpected occurrences whenever possible.

PERCENTAGE INCREASE INTRADAY

My scanner alerts me to stocks up by 40% or higher on the day. (The indicator is seasonal and occasionally I will raise the percentage to 75% or 100% on the day.) I focus on erratic securities—stocks that increase exponentially (squeeze). With this objective in mind, I check the news to observe the catalysts behind the prices—for example, wars or pandemics, which tend to attract the attention and excitement of buyers, boosting demand and driving up the stock price. I do not seek to compete with these global events. People all over the world buy the stock; this high demand creates uncertainty, which can potentially result in a black swan scenario—something I do my best to avoid. My

---

* Laila Maidan, "A Short Seller with a More Than 90% Win Ratio Shares the 9 Indicators That Make for a 'Beautiful Stock to Short,'" *Business Insider*, July 8, 2023.

motto is, 'Don't fight the crowd' (as I did with meme stocks in the early days).

NANO FLOATS

Avoid stocks under 1 million public floats—the total number of shares of a company's stock that are publicly available to trade. Manipulators target these stocks with tiny floats, which have the potential to squeeze exponentially with a small amount of volume (demand) and have a higher likelihood of manipulation of supply (float), as supply is low.

MARKET CAP

Avoid stocks over $250 million market cap because they are likely to be real companies with a higher probability of institutional ownership. Most likely, these companies are not blatantly dubious and are usually vetted. In contrast, companies under $250 million market cap typically exhibit certain characteristics:

- They are minuscule market caps, with borderline questionable practices. We know the endgame: most of them will eventually go to zero. In many instances, they don't have a product. They are constantly seeking capital and probably hoping to capitalize on any pump headline, raise cash, and dilute the shareholders for that purpose. Traders cannot trade based on these assumptions, however, as these companies will fight and find a way to survive in the markets. They will stay alive just long enough to raise cash, dilute, dump the shares, and repeat that activity continuously until they go to zero (which sometimes can take years longer than short sellers would believe).
- They don't sustain their gains for a long time (perhaps a few days or weeks at most).
- They eventually are delisted after diluting shareholders and

repeatedly raising cash and going through the reverse-split cycle multiple times over.

These types of scenarios are much easier to navigate for short sellers who seek to know the endgame. That is my reason for focusing on $250 million market caps or less, because the inevitable endgame is the stock's decline after significant runups. Two hundred and fifty million dollar market caps or less also classify as small-cap companies, which are more volatile and don't hold their gains very well. As fast as they go up, they usually come down just as hard—or harder. Larger companies don't behave in this fashion and don't provide the kind of volatility necessary to snowball smaller accounts into large ones over the long run. (For example, I took my $29,000 account to seven-plus figures in just a few years.)

The stock's price fades after a couple of months or even a couple of years, then goes to cents on the dollar. Each time the stock rises, I know it will eventually crash. So, I capitalize on that movement: the company will raise money to stay alive, dilute its shares and, as the stock descends to low ebbs, execute a reverse split. This is commonly known as a 'reverse-split cycle,' which inevitably repeats until the stock is delisted or goes to zero.

Therefore, investors do not remain in the stocks for long; and when they see an opportunity to profit as a result of an upward price spike, they will likely seize the chance to sell. Such opportunities for investors to profit are not commonplace. Typically, investors only have a few opportunities to profit before the stock irreversibly declines and fades into an endless reverse-split cycle. The stock requires volume and liquidity, but this occurs infrequently. That is what makes small caps predictable—they are highly likely to sell into liquidity events.

Investors in companies that match my short-selling criteria most likely will sell when there is opportunity for profit instead of holding long-term for a significant development (e.g., a cure for terminal illnesses). It is important to note that there are a few companies in the small-cap space that do not engage in questionable practices and have good management and product. However, that is an exceptional scenario.

In contrast, healthy companies don't engage in frequent reverse splits; they don't require constant cash; they don't engage in paid promotional campaigns and other factors that contribute to my short-selling checklist. Investors in these companies are more likely to be there for the long haul and will not sell immediately. (They sometimes wait years, seeking huge home-run wins.) I avoid shorting these companies. Many of them will have an intermittent extended intraday move. When this occurs and short sellers enter, the space becomes overcrowded because the investors hold out from selling their stock. No one is *truly* selling, and an outlier short squeeze potentially can result. That could last for many days, causing continuous spikes by forced buying. Note that this is not actual demand from excited buyers. This is a process of painful, forced buying as the shorts cover their positions.

In all likelihood, the news or catalyst is genuine and the stock's current trading price becomes the new stock price. In many instances, these companies have institutional ownership presence, which can be problematic for the short seller because of algorithms with an agenda supporting the stock price, and because institutions most likely have vetted the company.

INSTITUTIONAL OWNERSHIP PERCENTAGE

Avoid stocks over 40% institutional ownership, as it's highly likely that institutions have vetted such companies. These could be sophisticated funds with algorithms and institutions that have extremely large amounts of capital ready to buy and support the stock for their own agenda: to build a large position and squeeze short sellers. This is not hyperbole: I gained insight into the world of algorithms and institutions firsthand through my podcast interviews with industry experts.

STOCKS UNDER $1

Avoid shorting stocks under $1. Shorting these stocks takes too much capital. Some brokers require a $2.50 per share margin for each share, even if the stock is priced considerably lower. The reason: this helps limit risk, as low-priced stocks can be extremely volatile. For example, if you short 1,000 shares at $0.75, you will need $2,500 margin, even though the value of your position is only $750. Imagine if your position were larger—the amount required would be astronomical. You can put your capital to far greater use than getting involved with trading sub-dollar stocks and risking a squeeze. Shorting such stocks does not provide a positive risk-reward scenario. The key is to put your capital to more productive use.

Note that companies with failing stocks have an incentive to reach $1 to maintain their listing on the exchanges. Listing and delisting are very costly procedures and companies lose out on raising money from being on the exchanges if they get delisted. Most funds and investors only invest in listed stocks on major exchanges, such as Nasdaq and the NYSE. Therefore, companies are highly incentivized to drive up the stock price through whatever methods might serve their purposes—like press releases or other short-term fixes—so they can maintain the value of the company above the minimum level to remain on the exchanges. My preference is to avoid shorting stocks under $2. However, I adapt to the market's fluidity and the prevailing circumstances. I also take the risk-reward balance into account.

If a company is non-compliant, it eventually receives a letter from the exchange with a deadline for compliance and a hearing date. Many short sellers typically deem this filing to be negative news—an indication that the stock will be delisted. However, it's important not to short the company's stock solely because it is likely to receive an ongoing extension. Extensions sometimes create the impression of good news for the company. As a result, sudden increased demand for the stock ensues. In that case, buyers can enter and push up the stock price, contributing to a short squeeze. Note that the stock can continue in limbo with hearings and extensions for several 180-day intervals before the company actually is delisted.

BORROW FEE RATE

The borrow fee rate—the broker's annualized overnight fee for lending shorts to short sell—can be used as an intraday indicator of short interest rates. This is a way to reverse-engineer short interest on the stock, as short interest is only reported twice a month. By using the borrow fee rate as an indicator, short sellers can observe the demand for short selling per stock symbol on a daily or even hourly basis. I use Interactive Brokers Trader WorkStation (TWS) to monitor borrow fee rates. Borrow fee rates have increased steadily over the years. In the past, rates were lower, with a T+3 settlement cycle. However, since the SEC reduced the requirement to a T+1 settlement period due to the new 'T+1 rule', rates have risen exponentially and the short selling environment has changed—and we short sellers must adapt accordingly. Clearing firms have had difficulty adjusting to the new T+1 rule, which has led to a frenzy of squeezes, as short sellers don't want to hold overnight due to the outrageous fees charged for doing so.

The 'T+1 rule' refers to the settlement cycle for securities transactions. Under this rule, when a trade is executed, the settlement (i.e., the transfer of ownership and payment) occurs one business day (T+1) after the trade date (T). Here's a breakdown:

- 'T' stands for the 'trade date,' which is the day on which the transaction takes place.
- '+1' indicates that the settlement of the transaction will happen one business day after the trade date. For example, if an investor buys or sells a stock on Monday (the trade date), the settlement will occur on Tuesday (the next business day).

The purpose of the rule is to reduce settlement time and increase market efficiency. To compensate, I have tightened my entry criteria during market cycles that typically see increased squeeze activity. With the shift to T+1 settlement, the frequency and intensity of these squeezes have escalated—largely due to clearing firms struggling to adjust accordingly. As a result, I now set my entry threshold to focus on stocks showing 100% gains; and in particularly high-activity periods, I raise this threshold to 150% gainers for the day. This adjustment helps minimize the risk of entering shorts prematurely.

DILUTION

Look for potential dilution, which adds downward selling pressure to the stock. When a company dilutes its shareholders, the stock's value declines. An analogy is adding water to freshly squeezed orange juice, thus reducing its nutritional value. When the company has three months of cash or less, the probability is much higher that it will dip into other dilution reserves to pay bills (e.g., an at-the-market (ATM) offering or a cash raise with the bank). In this scenario, investors receive shares in the form of warrants or similar dilutive methods, often at a significant discount for immediate cash. They are likely to sell these shares promptly, taking advantage of the stock's temporarily higher trading price. If a company's stock does not indicate the potential for dilution or is over $250 million in market cap, that stock doesn't meet my criteria for a short position on significant news; it might present a strong case for a long position instead.

WARRANTS

I also keep an eye on warrants in a stock. Institutions and funds own the warrants and eventually look to cash them out for profit, which dilutes the stock. For the most part, individuals are not long-term investors but flippers who take advantage of the stock's volatility. I aim to short 30–50% above the warrant prices, where the warrant holders are most likely to exercise the warrants for a profit. The warrant holder profits only when the stock price rises reasonably above its selling price. I evaluate warrant ownership. If the owner is an institution or a well-known fund that is frequently involved in small-cap stocks, I anticipate it will sell off quickly once the price rises significantly above the warrant levels. If the owner is an individual, they may be holding the stock for the long term or may be unaware of the recent price surge due to infrequent monitoring. As a result, the stock may continue its upward trend.

HISTORICAL CHART

The historical chart performance should be examined and compared. There are multiple time frames within long-term charts. Pay attention to the intraday data by analyzing one-minute and five-minute candlesticks; then zoom out to examine the stock's one-year and multi-year performance for a comprehensive understanding. Some traders only examine intraday, but it's important to have a panoramic view of the stock's history.

LEVEL 2 BID AND ASK

Time and sales reflect executed asks and bids, fundamentally driven by supply and demand. This process mirrors an auction, where buyers and sellers align their orders. Exchanges do not determine prices; they simply facilitate transactions. As I read Level 2, I stare at the flickering screen to determine whether an algorithm is involved in the stock price's trajectory. Generally, I go by the size of the numbers. I'm looking for indicators of large 'iceberg orders,' which typically signal substantial sell-side activity. These are often orders from major sellers or companies executing share dilution, aiming to capitalize on temporary high-volume, high-liquidity events to offload shares. Similarly, warrant holders with substantial positions may seek to liquidate if the stock price exceeds their warrant exercise price, taking advantage of these liquidity surges. Such activity can be observed in Level 2 data as significant, layered orders that resemble iceberg orders, hinting at hidden supply intended to capitalize on the market's temporary liquidity. (See 'Tips and Tricks' below for expansion of this concept.) I also check to see if there is potential dilution. If a company has liquidity to dilute, I confirm my thesis with confidence. If the stocks show signs of dumping, such as significantly sized red candles following a series of green ones, I will short them. Once filled, these iceberg orders make the float bigger and more sluggish—an ideal scenario for a short seller to capitalize on the downward trajectory of the stock's price.

Note: Every short seller has access to Level 2 through their brokerage—typically with a fee. It's important to have this feature, so you can see more detail in the price action. In the past, Level 2 used to be accessible only to Wall Street professionals, but now every retail trader has that benefit.

INTRADAY-TRADER QUESTIONNAIRE

- What is the overall market environment like for small-cap stocks?
- What is the news?
- Why is the stock up on the day?
- Has the stock decreased over multiple years because of dilution?
- Has the company done reverse splits in the past?
- Who is likely on the other side of a trade?
- What is the company's likely agenda? Is the company trying to raise cash or dilute?
- Is the news or social media buzz influencing the stock's price action?
- Are these sources accurate/real or hyperbolic?

- Who owns the stock and do any of the owners raise a red flag?
- Is the company legitimate?
- Is there an institutional ownership presence in the company?
- Is there too much demand and insufficient supply?
- If there is no news, where is the demand coming from?
- Is the stock's price action organic (i.e., humans are buying and selling) or algorithmic (back-and-forth high-frequency trading at incomprehensibly excessive speeds)?

THE EFFICACY OF ENVISIONING TRADES— IT'S NOT ALL ABOUT REAL-TIME CHARTS

Although the intraday checklist is of vital importance, successful traders must envision their trades, much as fighter-jet pilots cognitively chart their course. They learn as much from envisioning as from hands-on application. Knowledge serves as a foundation for mapping out your plan of action so that, when confronted with actual trades, you have a basis for how to proceed and how to strategize your next move. (Another analogy is that of a game of chess.) Conceptualization must occur prior to and after the actual trade. When I first began my podcast, I had interviews and conversations similar to those in Seth's office in Puerto Rico. There weren't any visuals, such as charts or B-rolls, and that was fine for my purposes. I wanted to connect with traders/invitees to the podcast to gain hands-on experience and improve my game. In addition, I aimed to keep the podcast simple and minimalist without focusing on the requisites of podcasting. My primary objective was to exchange knowledge and ideas with like-minded people and enhance my skills as a trader—nothing more. My quest for knowledge facilitated my entry into the world of podcasting, and before I knew it, my podcasting skills developed organically. Without visuals, I had to intensely conjure up each trade in my mind—on the spot—during every high-level discussion. The process wasn't easy, but it was a worthy exercise and the best training ground.

A word to the wise

Perfect practice

When looking at the charts, everyone invariably deconstructs what they see. That is, they interpret what they want to see on the charts and make erroneous projections about what is happening. This kind of learning is not productive at all, since the viewer isn't breaking down the trade into its component parts. For example, without the charts on audio podcasts (as was the case for me), traders are forced to use their cognitive abilities to decipher any given trading concepts discussed between the podcast host and the guests. Over time, this process incrementally hones the skills conducive to perfect practice and success in trading. A key element of perfect practice involves going back and listening to the podcast multiple times to reinforce the lessons learned and probe into those concepts that you don't understand. I applied this approach both in my own podcast and as an avid listener of other podcasts.

Best-selling author and renowned trader Tom Hougaard and I discussed this vital 'perfect practice' during my annual *Friendly Bear* conference in Los Angeles on October 10, 2025. Tom emphasized the importance of full cognitive engagement during practice, not simply mindless observation without conceptualization or probing. To be fully immersed in trading, you must question, analyze, and go over every lesson with an open mind and the understanding that you learn more through review and repetition.

Perfect practice also involves simulation of actual events. As Tom pointed out, the father of famed golfer Tiger Woods used to rattle coins in a can while his son practiced, simulating the actual environment of a golf tournament. Tiger's father prepared him for the distractions that are all around golfers on a competition course, so he could perform optimally at each event.

The takeaway: don't simply look at a trade mindlessly. Engage in perfect practice by delving into the trade and your actions and reactions within it—why you may have broken rules and how you could have navigated it differently. Journaling facilitates this process. No scenario is black or white; you must break down the trade consistently and analyze your process within it.

FOREIGN VERSUS DOMESTIC STOCKS

If something is beyond my understanding, that is a red flag. There are higher odds of a possible outlier, such as the way stocks from China behave: they trade erratically and are prone to volatile price action as they are heavily manipulated from overseas.

Domestic stocks tend to adhere more closely to regulations, or at least a significant portion of them. In contrast, foreign stocks may more readily bypass these rules, making them a favored target for manipulators who engage in aggressive tactics, particularly to create risky short squeezes. How can I, as a retail trader, compete against foreigners who could be in any corner of the world using dubious, untraceable tactics—all while immune to regulation outside U.S. jurisdiction? That's why I strive to always understand my competition.

LESSONS LEARNED

STICK TO THE PROCESS

Have conviction about the stocks you trade and follow the 'pilot's preflight checklist.' If you don't have conviction about a given stock, it's best not to trade at all.

PAY ATTENTION TO THE SIX MOST SALIENT STOCK CRITERIA

- **Market cap (small-cap companies with weaker financial performances)**: These companies may be trying to maintain Nasdaq compliance, have insider trading, or be engaging in price manipulations as short-term hype due to positive news. There are more opportunities each day with small-cap stocks than with mid or large-cap stocks, which have relatively less volatility and price movements for short-term trading. Greater volatility affords short sellers more opportunities to grow their accounts. This awareness, coupled with strict rules and confidence in your process, helps obliterate FOMO. Following and sticking to proven rules without deviation is the key to success.
- **Float**: This tells us how many shares are publicly available to trade in the market (i.e., stock supply). I look for stocks with a float of over 2 million. The lower the float, the more squeeze potential it has, since the supply is lower. Price fluctuations most often occur when a float is low. Larger players can accidentally or even purposefully take a big position in the stock and most of the supply when doing so. This can lead to more violent squeezes as short sellers crowd themselves in the stock. At all costs, avoid a short squeeze, which occurs when the price surges and there is no opportunity to exit to cut your losses. Therefore, the higher the float, the more tradable it is. However, pay heed to excessive float height, as it will move too sluggishly—the supply will be too large. I look for the sweet spot: somewhere between 5 and 20 million public float, with the potential for the float to increase with incoming dilution due to the company's cash need.
- **News**: News speaks volumes and testifies to cause and effect. What causes a stock to gap up in the morning? Is it recycled news that has already been published? What would others think of this news? Is it credible? How would long-biased and short-biased traders

respond? Determine whether the news generates genuine demand to drive the stock higher, particularly as short sellers are forced to cover their positions. This often occurs when they miscalculate the impact of mergers and acquisitions, dividend announcements, or complex partnership details with larger companies—key indicators of bullish price movement.

- **Company revenues and dilution history**: Typically, engaging in dilution means the company is weak and needs cash. It issues offerings such as private placements and secondary offerings. This exerts selling pressure on the stock (dilution). Use AskEdgar to gain an edge in fundamental research.
- **Sector**: The stock niche is an important indicator of whether to trade a given stock. At times, biotechs have a propensity to surge exponentially without any reason or noticeable stock pattern. It's not predictable and can't be calculated.
- **Stocks from countries and regions of dubious or unregulated origin**: These should also be avoided, as they are susceptible to manipulation from overseas, given the lack of SEC rule enforcement outside the U.S. Certain foreign stocks should be completely avoided, such as those with Chinese ties. Other foreign stocks should be handled with caution.

TIPS AND TRICKS

UTILIZE RELIABLE TOOLS STRATEGICALLY:

- **Trade Ideas**: Set up visual cues like flags to immediately identify a stock's country of origin. Pair these with detailed analysis for foreign stocks to avoid surprises.
- **Dilution Tracker**: Always verify the results against Trade Ideas, particularly for stocks with misleading domiciles (e.g., FNGR).

- **Proprietary bots**: Customize criteria to filter out undesirable stocks. For foreign-related concerns, scrutinize board member profiles and insider activity.
- **AskEdgar**: Leverage AI to identify foreign business dealings, particularly with China, which might introduce higher risks.

MASTER YOUR RESOURCES AND UNDERSTAND STOCK ORIGIN AND DOMICILE:

- **Double-check sources**: Ensure every piece of data, from domiciles to dilution potential, aligns across multiple tools. Missteps can cost dearly, as evidenced by the FNGR incident.
- **Understand relationships**: A stock may not be domiciled in China but could have significant business dealings or insider ties, warranting caution.

REFINE TRADE SELECTION:

- **Stick to criteria**: Avoid nano float stocks under 1 million or those with market caps over $250 million. Lower market caps often align better with short-sell strategies, as they are more volatile and inefficient. This means that they can capitulate faster when they are extended. As short sellers, we look to capitalize on this scenario. On the other hand, the bigger market caps move slower and don't provide as many opportunities for short sellers, as they trade more efficiently.
- **Institutional ownership**: Steer clear of stocks with over 40% institutional presence; algorithms and funds could build a position and squeeze out the shorts aggressively.
- **Stay agile with borrow fee rates**: Monitor overnight borrow fee rates, which update hourly on Interactive Brokers TWS to reverse-engineer short-interest trends. High borrow fee rates often signal increased demand for short selling.
- **Avoid red flags with foreign stocks**: Be wary of erratic trading behavior and potential for manipulation in overseas jurisdictions. Domestic stocks generally adhere more to regulations, reducing unpredictability.

PLAN FOR MARKET FLUIDITY:

- Adjust criteria during volatile market cycles (e.g., increase thresholds for percentage gainers).
- Avoid shorting stocks under $1, as companies may resort to aggressive tactics to maintain listing compliance.
- **Watch for dilution signals**: Look for signs like warrants being exercised or cash raises. These often lead to downward price pressure.
- **Historical perspective matters**: Use multi-year charts alongside intraday data to contextualize stock behavior.
- **Continuously learn and adapt**: Stay informed about regulatory changes, such as the T+1 rule, and adapt strategies accordingly to mitigate risks like short squeezes.

Chapter 9

PATENT NEWS: A CLASSIC PUMP-AND-DUMP CATALYST

PATENT NEWS IS a classic pump-and-dump catalyst, often used in the stock market, particularly for small-cap companies. This chapter highlights the effect of patent news on the market, its classic pump-and-dump pattern, and the tactics that affect after-hours market dynamics. I provide examples of the movement of these stocks, such as HOTH Therapeutics Inc. (HOTH) in the biotech sector. HOTH's precipitous surge was likely manufactured for investors to liquidate, creating an opportunity for short sellers to capitalize. Evaxion A/S (EVAX) attracted volume right after market close from buyers who use breaking news algorithms, causing a dramatic spike, followed by seller liquidation.

Autonomix Medical, Inc. (AMIX) was an anomaly for my patent news strategy, as it released patent news in the premarket and threw off my timing. This taught me to only consider shorting a stock that is 100% or more up on the day during the premarket. Avinger, Inc. (AVGR) demonstrated that patent news with potential tight halt bands can be tradable as long as tight halt bands don't get in the way. However, it's better to short in the premarket without the presence of tight halt bands because these can be highly manipulated in the regular hours.

THE PITFALLS OF PATENTS

Elon Musk—arguably, one of the most brilliant businesspeople of our time—has criticized patents, arguing that they often block innovation rather than promote it. Many struggling companies exploit patents as a short-term catalyst to inflate their stock prices. This tactic is commonly used by companies seeking to raise cash or dilute their shares. Small-cap companies, in particular, time these announcements strategically—typically at the 4 p.m. EST market close, when after-hours trading begins. The after-hours market has lower liquidity, wider bid-ask spreads (which can be manipulated more easily), and fewer active participants—especially large institutional short sellers, which typically trade only during regular market hours. As a result, the stock price can spike with relatively low demand due to the thin order book.

The companies using this tactic are aware of after-hours trading dynamics. They release patent news not because it signals meaningful innovation but because it can create a brief surge in the stock price, allowing insiders and dilution holders to offload shares. Patent news is generally a weak catalyst and seasoned traders recognize this as a red flag. However, desperate companies use it as a short-term fix to pacify unhappy insiders and investors. Disgruntled shareholders often put pressure on management to 'do something' to boost the stock price. In response, CEOs resort to speculative announcements or promises of 'exciting news' to spark optimism. When patent news drops, it attracts retail buyers: breaking-news algorithms entice people to buy indiscriminately, creating temporary liquidity that allows insiders to sell their shares before the inevitable collapse.

The pattern is predictable: patent news is announced, the stock price spikes, dilution holders sell into the pump, and bag-holders are left holding the stock as it plummets. It's a classic pump-and-dump cycle where the winners are those who understand the game, plan, and exit early, while unsuspecting retail investors bear the losses. Traders should be cautious when they see patent announcements, especially from struggling small-cap companies, as they often are a signal of insider maneuvers rather than genuine innovation or long-term value.

HOTH'S PATENT NEWS AND MARKET REACTION

Patent announcements often drive significant stock movements, especially in the biotech sector, but this behavior also extends beyond the industry. A clear example occurred with HOTH (a company devising a treatment for Alzheimer's disease) on November 19, 2024, when the company released patent news, triggering a sharp spike in its stock price.

The stock surged rapidly, reaching a high of $1.23 within minutes as buyers—including algorithmic trading bots programmed to react to news catalysts—piled in. However, the spike was short-lived. Investors quickly sold off their positions, driving the stock back down to $0.82 by the close of the following trading day—effectively returning to its starting point.

From a short seller's perspective, this was a classic example of a pump-and-dump-style reaction to news. Larger players capitalized on the surge by liquidating their positions into the buying frenzy, creating a perfect alignment for short sellers to enter and profit from the rapid reversal.

This event highlights a common pattern: when short sellers align their moves with the bigger players' liquidation strategies, they can effectively capitalize on the sharp rise and fall driven by news-based market reactions.

Figure 2: HOTH 5-minute chart showing patent news pump

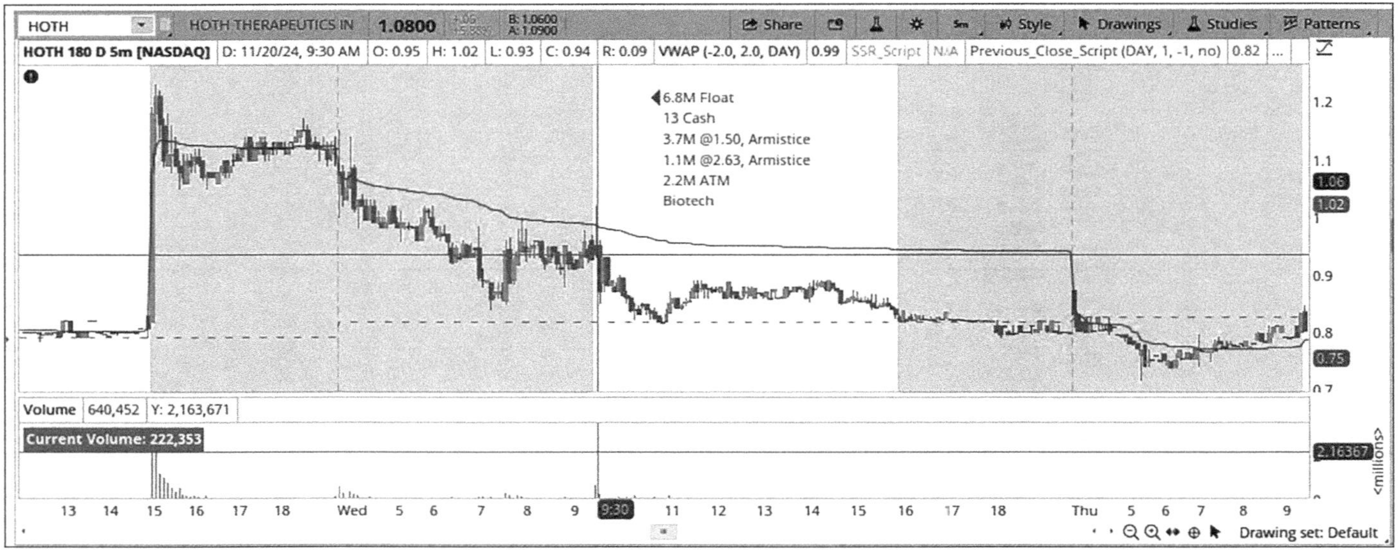

Source: Charles Schwab, thinkorswim® (TOS) software.

EVAX STOCK MOVEMENT ANALYSIS

On December 26–27, 2024, during after-hours trading, EVAX (a company developing a vaccine targeting *Neisseria gonorrhoeae*) announced significant patent news, causing the stock to spike 140% immediately. Similar to the pattern observed with HOTH, this announcement likely attracted buyers, including those using algorithms and breaking-news-based strategies. However, the surge was quickly met with selling pressure as larger players liquidated their positions into the demand.

As mentioned, short sellers typically align their positions with these major sellers, contributing to the natural downward price action. Consequently, despite the dramatic after-hours spike, the stock closed the following trading day near its original starting price.

Figure 3: EVAX 5-minute chart showing patent news pump

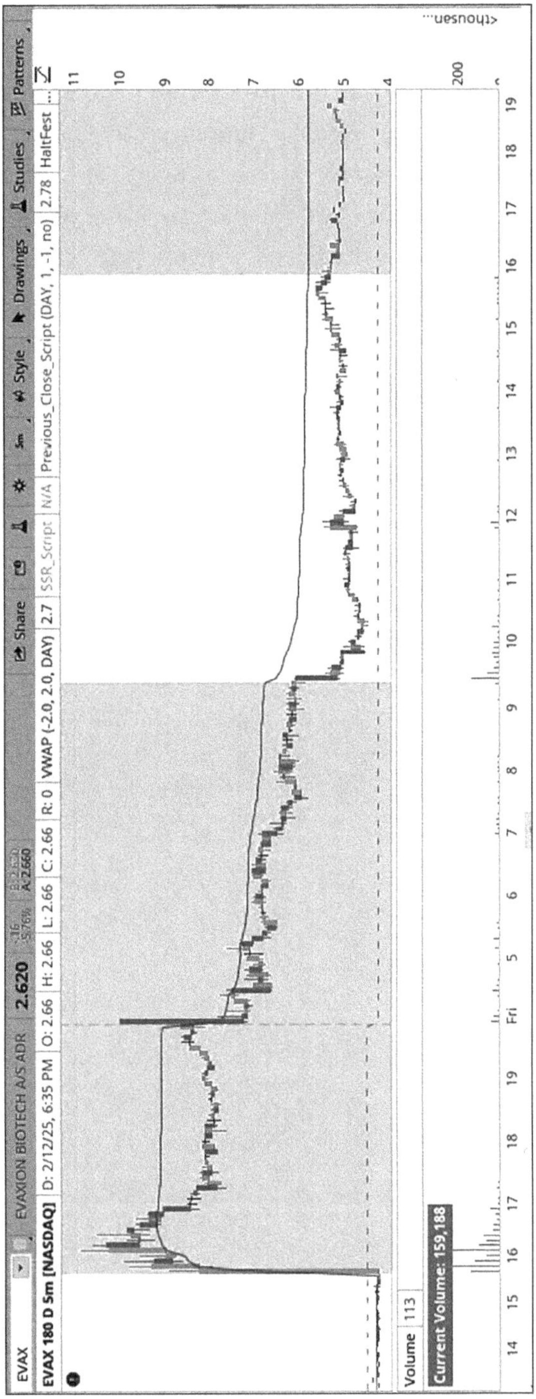

Source: Charles Schwab, thinkorswim® (TOS) software.

AMIX

AMIX is always on my radar for a potential short sell, provided the float isn't extremely low (nano float). The key is patience: waiting until the stock completes its upward run. This stock is rarely observed in the premarket.

The timing of AMIX's release of patent news—8:30 a.m. EST on December 30, 2024—was an anomaly that threw off my patent news strategy, which is mostly contingent on after-hours timing. Patent news is typically released at market close. The likely reason for releasing patent news at that time is to use it as a catalyst for pumping the stock in the presence of less liquidity. Patent news is generally a weak catalyst, and if it were released at market open, it would probably be ineffective. To avoid such situations, I now follow strict criteria:

- Only consider shorting if the stock is up 100% or more on the day during the premarket.
- Premarket carries significant risk for short squeezes due to increased volume, as brokers open for trading every hour, on the hour, between 7 and 9 a.m. EST. This period often sees a surge in volume from traders participating before their workday. The aim is to cover the position at the end of day, with the cover target being the beginning of the initial runup price. This is the ideal scenario.

Figure 4: AMIX 5-minute chart showing patent news pump

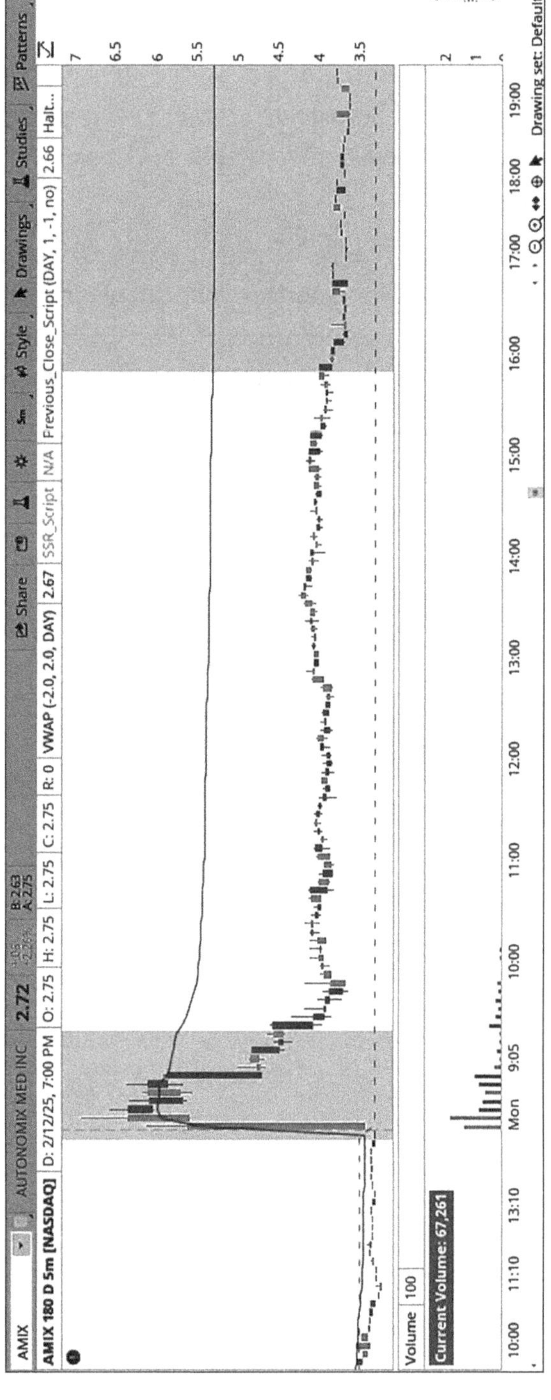

Source: Charles Schwab, thinkorswim® (TOS) software.

TIGHT HALT BAND RULE

On December 24, 2024, AVGR decided to give itself an early Christmas gift, causing a sharp spike in its stock price from $0.60 to $2.60 (a massive 300% increase) due to patent news. The company used this opportunity to liquidate shares into the price spike, capitalizing on the sudden demand.

A word to the wise

Tight halt bands are circuit breaker levels that pause trading if a stock's price moves too far, too fast. Stocks that close the day before below $0.75 and open above this level the next day are especially prone to halts, for the following reasons:

- **Less price range triggers a halt**: The price moves quickly beyond the threshold.
- **Increased volatility**: Small-cap or penny stocks with a low float can easily be manipulated into short squeezes.

THE UNFOLDING OF AVGR'S PATENT PLAY

The stock closed under $0.75 the previous day but opened above this level the next morning. By 10:45 a.m. EST on December 24, 2024, it spiked again. Predictably, inexperienced long traders chased the upward momentum. Then, the stock quickly hit resistance, rejected the volume weighted average price (VWAP) area, and failed to halt, even though the halt bands were tight. This indicated heavy selling.

Note that tight halt bands occur during market open, not during the premarket hours.

To halt, the price must remain at the halt price level for ten seconds before the exchange halts it. As a bearish trader, I sometimes observe the stock price rise to just shy of ten seconds before it dumps, which indicates active selling pressure into the halt levels. Traders can observe this on Level 2 on the Limit Down, Limit Up (LDLU) indicator. If the stock price hits the LDLU in either direction, the exchange automatically halts the stock from trading, due to volatility. This is called a T-1 volatility halt, which typically lasts for five minutes or longer, depending on how long it takes for the exchange to match the buy and sell orders together.

As to AVGR, the tight halt bands did not get in the way of the price action, which made the stock tradable as a re-short for those who opted to do so. However, if a stock has tight halt bands, the premarket cover suffices for me—in this case, there was enough 'meat on the bone,' as the short was $2.50 with a $1.50 cover in the premarket. Therefore, there was no need to risk a potential tight halt band headache scenario.

The float was 3 million, but the company had over 10 million warrants and convertibles to dilute. Mostly likely, the company used the runup—consisting of various forms of dilution—on the patent news to achieve its aims and dump all the dilution.

Note: I usually avoid stocks that close the prior day under $0.75 and open up higher the next day; but for patent news situations that align with my other criteria, I will make an exception, since the strategy works so well.

KEY INSIGHTS FOR TRADERS

- **Premarket strategy**: This type of manipulated squeeze often crashes before the market opens. So, it's smarter to play the fade only in premarket, anticipating the fall, and avoid the tight halt bands once the market opens.
- **Shorting the squeeze**: When the stock spikes over VWAP during the trading session, this is an opportunity to enter another short position and ride the price back down to the close.

UNDERSTANDING THE MANIPULATION

Just as companies engage in other forms of manipulation (discussed earlier), AVGR used positive news (a patent announcement) to artificially drive demand, allowing insiders or institutions to sell their shares at inflated prices ('throwing a bone' to investors).

Retail traders and inexperienced short sellers often get caught in the squeeze, leading to forced covering (which drives the price up further before the eventual collapse). The company benefits by pacifying angry investors with news-driven excitement, allowing insiders to exit their positions at a premium.

In the case of AVGR, the long-term chart was basically a landslide and faced delisting. So, investors desperately wanted to exit.

TAKEAWAY ON THE TIGHT HALT BAND RULE

The tight halt band rule highlights how low-priced stocks, when they rise above critical halt thresholds, halt quickly due to volatility and become prime targets for manipulation.

With patent news, it's best to avoid the regular hours if tight halt bands are present. However, if the trade occurs premarket or after hours only, it's important to cover your position before the markets open, when the tight halt bands will take effect again.

Figure 5: AVGR 5-minute chart showing patent news pump, 2024

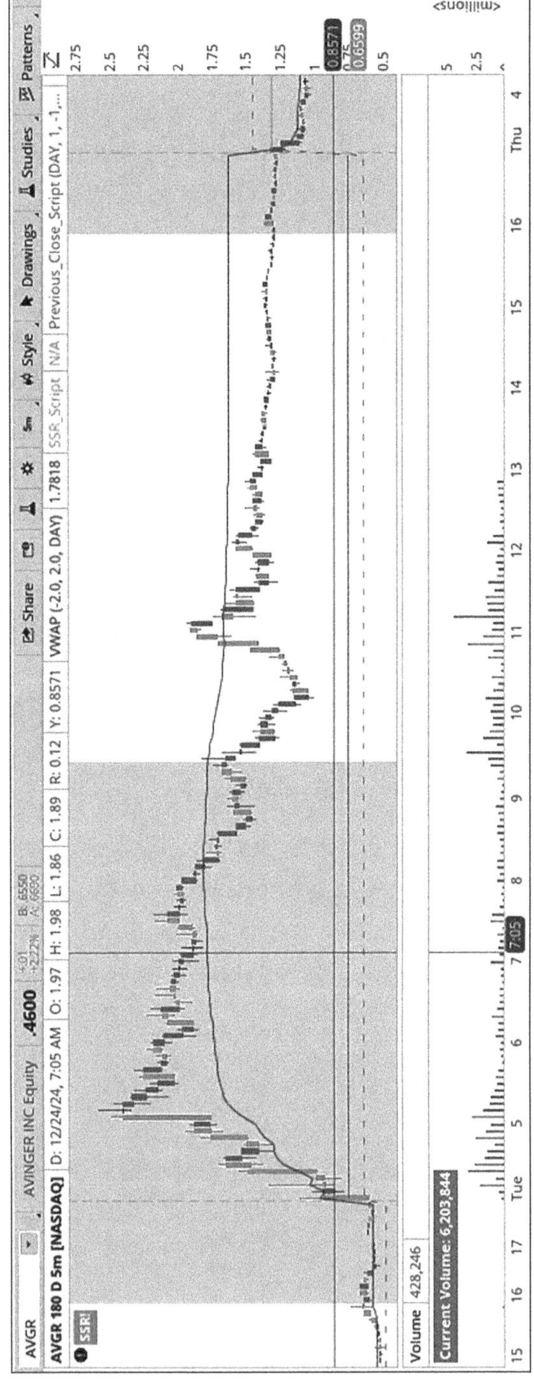

Source: Charles Schwab, thinkorswim® (TOS) software.

THE AFTERMATH

AVGR is another classic example of pump-and-dump manipulation, with its own playbook of patent moves. The company was on the verge of bankruptcy per public information—as traders can clearly observe in the SEC filings. The company is based in the U.S. and must be fully accountable under the law, unlike dubious foreign entities that are listed on the stock market. Almost two weeks after its first announcement of patent news, on January 13, 2024, the stock squeezed 115% into the close for dilution and liquidation to occur. For five to ten minutes, the stock spiked precipitously, then plummeted, giving disgruntled investors a chance to exit.

Most likely, the float had increased since AVGR's patent news runup and the company used the patent news to facilitate dilution. In February 2025, the company was voluntarily dissolved and underwent a liquidation and distribution process as an alternative to formal bankruptcy.

Figure 6: AVGR 5-minute chart showing patent news pump, 2025

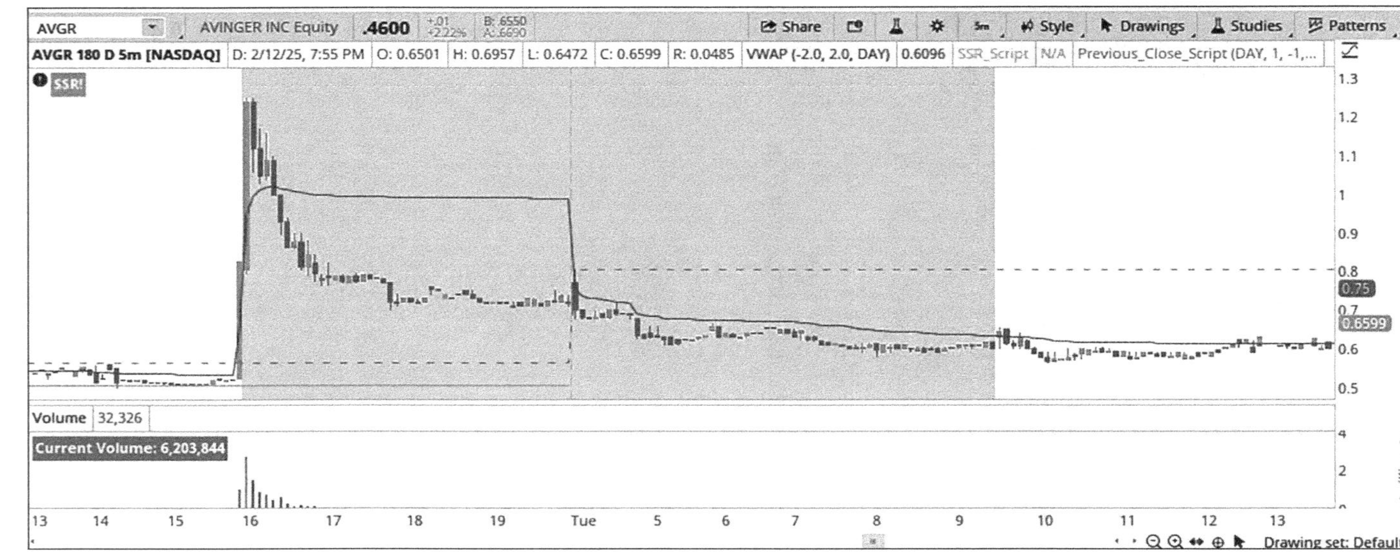

Source: Charles Schwab, thinkorswim® (TOS) software.

LESSONS LEARNED

PATENT NEWS MANIPULATION IS A QUINTESSENTIAL PUMP-AND-DUMP SCHEME

Patent announcements, especially from struggling small-cap companies, often signal pump-and-dump schemes rather than genuine innovation.

AFTER-HOURS TRADING RISKS

The absence of liquidity in the after-hours market renders trading susceptible to price manipulation.

RECOGNIZE DILUTION PATTERNS

Companies often use patent news to mask share dilution and insider selling.

PREMARKET SHORTING STRATEGY

Premarket spikes, especially from weak news-based catalysts, often crash after the market opens.

ALGORITHMIC TRADING INFLUENCE

Bots can cause rapid price spikes due to breaking news, but these are often short-lived because—especially in the small-cap space—the bots are largely designed to buy because of random breaking news. Companies are aware of this tendency and attempt to lure the bots to buy with weak breaking news (e.g., patent news).

VWAP RESISTANCE

Stocks have a higher probability of fading after hitting VWAP following a squeeze. It is a key area of resistance, as well as support. If the price surges over VWAP and then retraces its trajectory downward, the VWAP can act as a key support level.

TIGHT HALT BAND RULE AWARENESS

Stocks crossing tight halt bands due to volatility are prime targets for manipulation and can be difficult to trade, as they can halt erratically and repeatedly.

TIPS AND TRICKS

- **Do not chase news-based spikes**: Wait for the pattern to develop.
- **Focus on high-probability setups**: Short after major spikes, especially when dilution signs are present.
- **Use VWAP as a guide**: Seek to enter shorts if the price rejects VWAP after a spike.
- **Avoid premarket shorts without a setup**: The premarket is very risky because there is less liquidity, there are no halts, and stop losses are not available. So, you must monitor the trade and be able to exit it yourself.
- When a stock rises over 100% in the premarket, I wait for the first five-minute red candle to enter. I go through my process beforehand, asking the following questions:
    - o What is the float?
    - o What is the news?

- o What sector is the stock in? I don't want to be blindsided by those who are buying ahead of me and know the news beforehand—I check the news from multiple sources.
- o Did a filing go out the day before?
- o Then, I check to see if the stock went up over 100%, and when the first five-minute candle sets in and crosses the VWAP, I'll look to enter.

- **Monitor tight halt bands**: Be cautious around tight halt bands, which indicate extreme volatility.
- **Follow institutional moves**: Pay attention to price action that suggests insider or institutional selling.
- **Track company history**: Be wary of companies with a pattern of news-based pumps.
- **Watch volume trends**: In the case of patent news only, sudden high volume without substance often precedes a fade.
- **Learn from previous plays**: Study past cases (e.g., HOTH, EVAX, AVGR) to identify repeating patterns.
- **Stay disciplined**: Stick to your trading plan and risk management rules.

Chapter 10

DISCRETIONARY TRADER'S PLAYBOOK

IN THIS CHAPTER, I discuss what I consider to be prime shorting opportunities, following specific rules and patterns. Most notably, I reveal my strategies for identifying classic pump and dumps, based on my criteria—namely, companies in need of cash, a pattern of dilution and reverse splits, pervasive news catalysts and press releases, and the cyclical nature of short selling. I also focus on how to formulate a thesis about a given company, based on these observations.

Further, I highlight how to spot FRD patterns and the criteria associated with shorting stocks that exhibit these patterns.

PATTERNS INDICATIVE OF PUMP AND DUMPS

Unlike systematic traders who follow predefined rules, I carefully assess multiple factors before entering a trade. Through experience, I have identified patterns in certain stocks—particularly those lacking fundamental strength and legitimacy—that signal an inevitable decline. These characteristics make them prime candidates for repeated short selling over time when they pop up and meet my criteria along their probable downward trajectory toward eradication. Examples include

FLGC, Mullen Automotive, Inc. (MULN), Brera Holdings PLC, (BREA), and NXTP. (At the time of writing, NXTP has been delisted, but the concepts introduced below apply to manipulated stocks with the same dilutive reverse-split cycle.)

Occasionally, stocks from my playbook resurface during a common reverse-split setup and become overextended. Due to my strict criteria, designed to prevent me from shorting too early, I often become aware of these stocks during the middle or end of their runup. These potential trades often occur in tandem with FRD patterns. An FRD pattern occurs when a stock has risen significantly over several days due to a combination of hype and short squeezes, followed by a day when it closes lower than its opening after experiencing strong, fast upward momentum. Typically, before the FRD confirmation, the stock will have a 'blow-off top' (i.e., a last squeeze-out) before it ultimately dumps for a confirmed FRD. When the stock initially shows signs that an FRD is imminent, this often leads to panic selling as traders rush to exit their positions. Typically, in this scenario, the stock will decline 20% or more on the day.

Case studies of prime short-selling opportunities that follow my playbook of the dilutive reverse-split cycle include the following.

SAFETY SHOT, INC.

Safety Shot, Inc. (SHOT) (IPO: November 20, 2020) manufactures an energy drink sold in small bottles, purportedly designed to reduce blood alcohol content and alleviate hangover symptoms. In fact, it is like snake oil: a dubious miracle 'cure' that does absolutely nothing to facilitate the inebriation recovery process. Nothing can do that but time and subsequent abstinence from alcohol. People do not want to believe this truth, but so it is.

Figure 7: SHOT 5-minute chart showing patent news pump

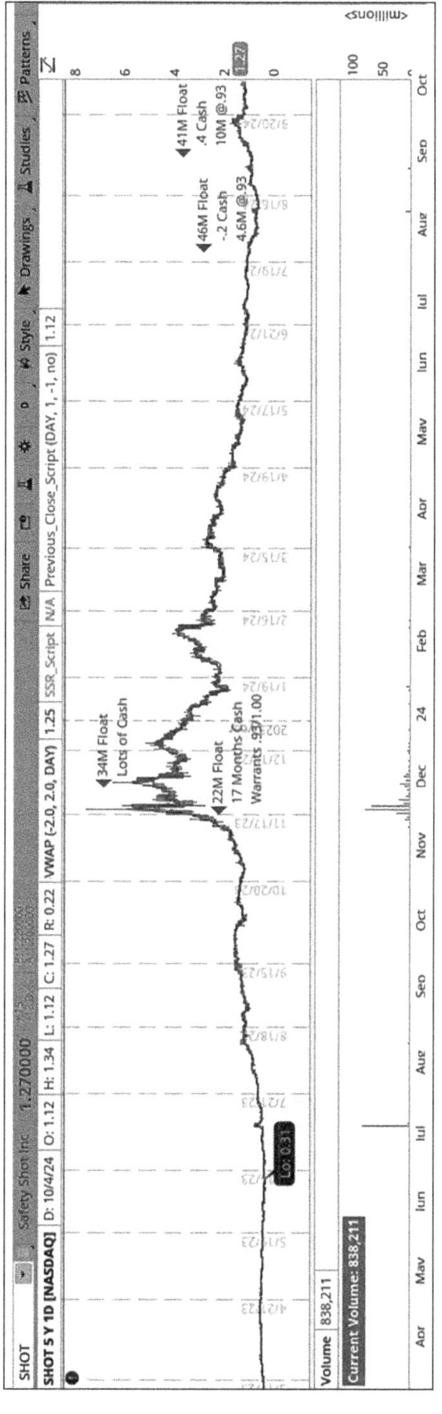

Source: Charles Schwab, thinkorswim® (TOS) software.

SHOT appeared during the Thanksgiving holiday in 2023 and had a significant run. Note that the holidays provide opportunities for kitchen-table conversations about stocks as many people indulge in festivities and consumerism. Pump and dumps typically thrive in an environment where most people are in a celebratory state. The time interval between Thanksgiving and the New Year is usually referred to as 'the Santa run.' Most people are in impetuous purchasing mode and are more vulnerable to companies that make grandiose promises but likely have dubious intentions to run up their stock price and cash out. This makes for an excellent shorting opportunity.

Enter yours truly. I traded SHOT on its classic FRD pattern. For more than a week leading up to Thanksgiving, the stock rose precipitously. Then, on November 22, the stock experienced its true FRD after it became overextended and unsustainable during the last phase of the runup. This most likely signaled that the pumpers manipulating the stock had begun to sell en masse, triggering panic selling among people who had not done their due diligence and had fallen prey to paid promotional campaigns and other hype. This is a timeless pump-and-dump pattern that historically repeats, particularly during the biggest holiday season of the year. In this environment, there is a higher probability of an FRD pattern, as these true A+ setups can occur only a few times a year. Notably, SHOT plummeted almost 60% on November 22, 2023—three days before Thanksgiving. (This goes to show that pumpers are typically unfazed by the impact of their actions on others.) Note that most FRD patterns are characterized by a negative 20% or more decline on the day.

One year later, the stock went down; and these days, it's a short every time: it goes up 40% on the day and no one anticipates anything—the secret is out and it's no longer exciting. These conditions are conducive to a consistently profitable trading strategy. Short sellers should always be aware of patterns that can lead to potentially profitable strategies that can become a consistent part of your playbook—and your longevity.

A word to the wise

Never accept stock tips from anyone. Unfortunately, there are people who want to enter the stock market without first doing their research. They simply want to make money quickly and buy because of hype. But there are no trading shortcuts. Many people innocently fall for erroneous trading advice—a natural consequence of groupthink, a psychological phenomenon that sometimes leads to conformity and trading disasters.

AN IN-DEPTH EXPLANATION OF FRD PATTERNS

The initial indication of an FRD occurs when stocks surge by 100% or more over multiple days. However, this is not a precise rule, since the FRD also depends on how far the stock extends on the chart over that time period. Eventually, an FRD will occur; but beforehand, it typically squeezes out the early shorts in a 'blow-off-top' scenario, followed by capitulation (i.e., a steep rise, followed by a sharp decline in the stock). For example, AMC (mentioned in Chapter 2) experienced an exponential surge during the meme stock bubble in early June 2021. During such bubbles, it's important to watch out for FRD patterns, as these periods are characterized by high volatility, with exponential surges and precipitous crashes almost a regular occurrence.

After its first few days, AMC set up for an FRD pattern. In cases such as this, the euphoria is unsustainable; when we start to see the hype reversing, with a corresponding decrease in volume, this indicates that demand is fading and the stock has likely reached its climax. That is a great FRD predictive indicator.

We must ask ourselves: 'Has the stock price gapped down recently?' If it has never gapped down in its runup and this is the first time, we must trust the odds of an FRD occurrence. Sometimes that is not the case and the stock gaps up. However, if it suddenly moves down after gapping up, we immediately can assume that, statistically speaking, an FRD is in the cards.

However, if the stock gaps down too much (e.g., by 20%, which would be a good point to cover), you shouldn't try to size into its weakness. If you keep adding to a short position during the FRD setup and the stock bounces strongly against you, once you're at full size, you'll most likely be forced to cut the trade for a loss when the stock goes green on the day. At that point, the FRD pattern is no longer valid in the moment.

After the bounce is over, the stock can continue on its downward trajectory and the FRD pattern is still in play. However, if you sized in too aggressively too early and then had to cut your losses, you may no longer be able to participate in the larger move downward.

The key lesson: going in too big too soon can take you out of the trade before the actual move develops. If that happens, you must cut your losses and move on, rather than fighting the trade.

Conversely, if a stock is weak and you only have a partial starter position, this is not ideal. Consistent gap-ups over the course of a few days can be challenging because you don't know when the FRD is approaching. In this scenario, it's important to look for a huge momentum shift. For example, if a stock spikes in the morning, sustains that surge throughout the day, and holds the highs, this becomes a strong support level. If the stock climbs and then falls significantly, but is still slightly green on the day, this is a significant indicator of a momentum shift—even though the stock has not yet gone red—suggesting that the end of the runup is near and an FRD is imminent. The next day, if it has a low-to-high trajectory—a bounce from the low point, followed by a new morning low—it may be wise to put those odds in your favor in preparation for a short position and allow it to play out for an FRD pattern. Ideally, you can scale in at the failure point (under VWAP) and try to capitalize on the downward momentum.

Figure 8: AMC 5-minute chart showing patent news pump

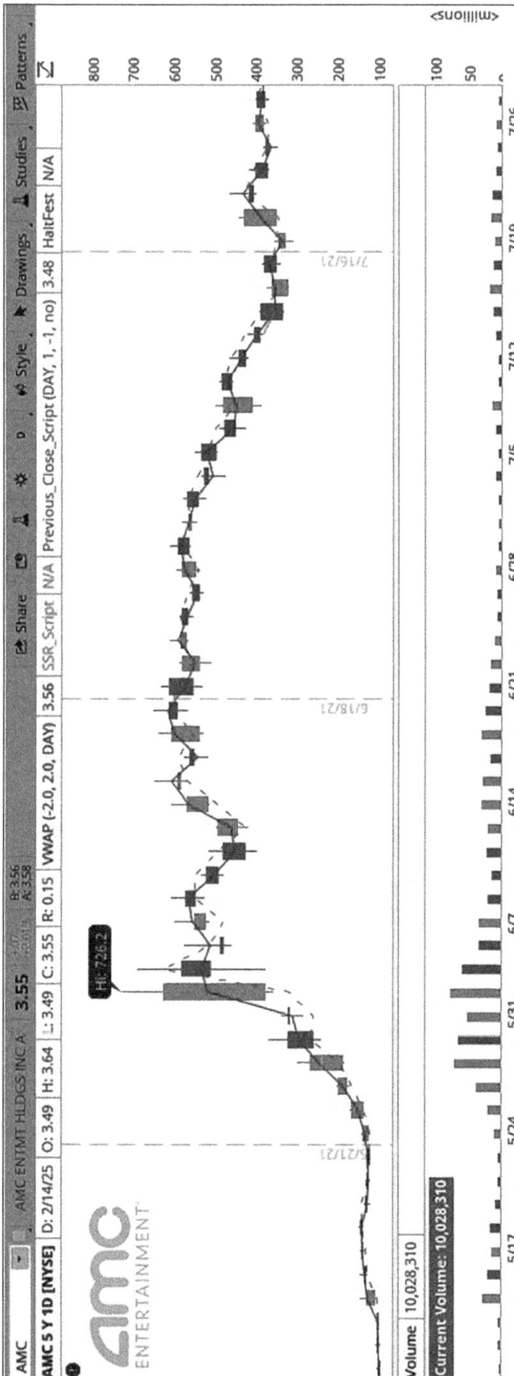

Source: Charles Schwab, thinkorswim® (TOS) software.

A word to the wise

Often, short sellers cover, which causes a surge in volume and attracts long traders to join in on the momentum, and the stock bounces back. This movement creates a secondary bounce (a 'bounce-short,' as I call it), and the short seller can re-short it into the resistance of the previous run. Thereafter, the stock will most likely experience smaller bounces (just as the bounces of a ball become increasingly weaker) and eventually fade into oblivion.

MOTORSPORT GAMES INC.

Motorsport Games Inc. (MSGM) (IPO: 2021), which specialized in game racing, did not capture anyone's imagination. Tied to promotional campaigns/pumps, texts, and emails over the course of a few years, it was always a short for me—that is, as long as it did not become a nano float and still satisfied my criteria. In October 2024 the stage was set and the stock was ripe for shorting. It was up more than 40% on the day; there was news of its inevitable decline; it had only three months of cash; it was a serial 'diluter'; and it had done a reverse split.

Figure 9: MSGM 5-minute chart showing patent news pump

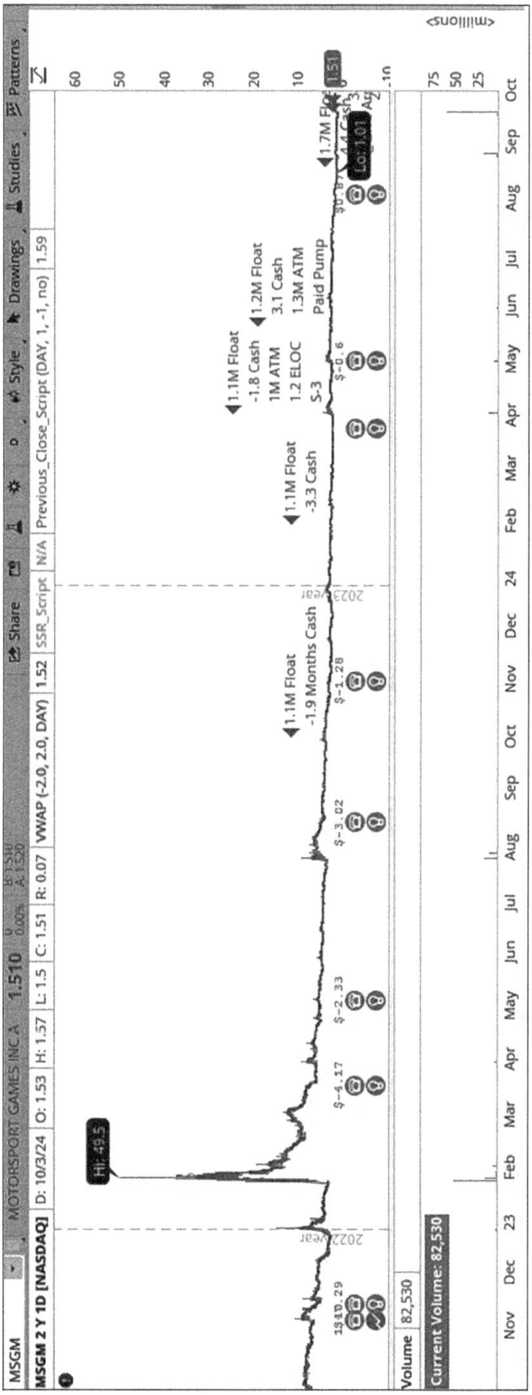

Source: Charles Schwab, thinkorswim® (TOS) software.

However, on January 31 and February 1, 2023, the stock was most likely heavily manipulated, since the supply was low and it was a nano float at the time. Significantly, it spiked up 2000% in two days (mostly in the premarket). One day previously, one of the stock's insiders (also an MULN insider) had reported 10% ownership. He held a big portion of the tiny float—the hallmark of a manipulative operation. Once the promotional text campaigns came out, the stock's decline was almost instantaneous. Since then, the company has done a reverse split, the float is now 1.6 million, and its warrants are at $2.17. Like its perpetually declining counterparts, the stock will continue to go through the reverse-split pump-and-dump cycle until it fades off entirely. It may even change its ticker name, just like MULN (previously NETE Element).

As of July 28, 2025, MULN—still an electric vehicle company—had changed its name and ticker symbol once again, to Bollinger Innovations (BINI). The ticker symbol change is likely intended to confuse traders—it throws people off. Since MULN has such a dubious reputation, it revised its name to evade scrutiny by short sellers and remain under the radar—at least for the time being.

A word to the wise

When a company changes its ticker symbol and company name, it is attempting to rehabilitate itself to reflect a new identity—a red flag for the veteran trader. Historically, dubious companies use this tactic to confuse traders and escape detection by short sellers, because short sellers will continue to apply downward pressure on the stock price as the supply increases over time. For a short time, while people remain unaware of the company's true identity, it can enjoy a brief period of obscurity as insiders and management devise a new strategy.

KNIGHTSCOPE INC.

Knightscope Inc. (KSCP) designs and manufactures autonomous security robots, focusing on public safety and security. Its IPO occurred in late January 2022, when I was still in Puerto Rico. Steve, my mentor, deemed it a questionable operation which could never replace human security—and he was right. I had seen at least one of the company's products in downtown LA while traveling to and from my office every six weeks or so from Puerto Rico. In an outdoor mall stood a robot resembling R2-D2, one of the iconic characters from the *Star Wars* films. It looked like a giant toy and appeared to have become immobilized in a random section of the mall. Always observant and in tune with my surroundings, I approached a security guard and inquired why the automaton was standing inert. Apparently, its battery had run low and it was unable to return to its charging mat. The device cost tens of thousands of dollars, yet it could not even do its job.

It bears mentioning that the people of downtown LA cared as much about such robots as they did about pigeons perched on statues—they were completely indifferent to them. No one felt safer with the robots around and many saw them as more of an entertaining novelty than a practical security measure. It thus became clear to me that these machines were more about the illusion of progress than the delivery of any real value in public safety.

Figure 10: KSCP daily chart depicting constant fader over time

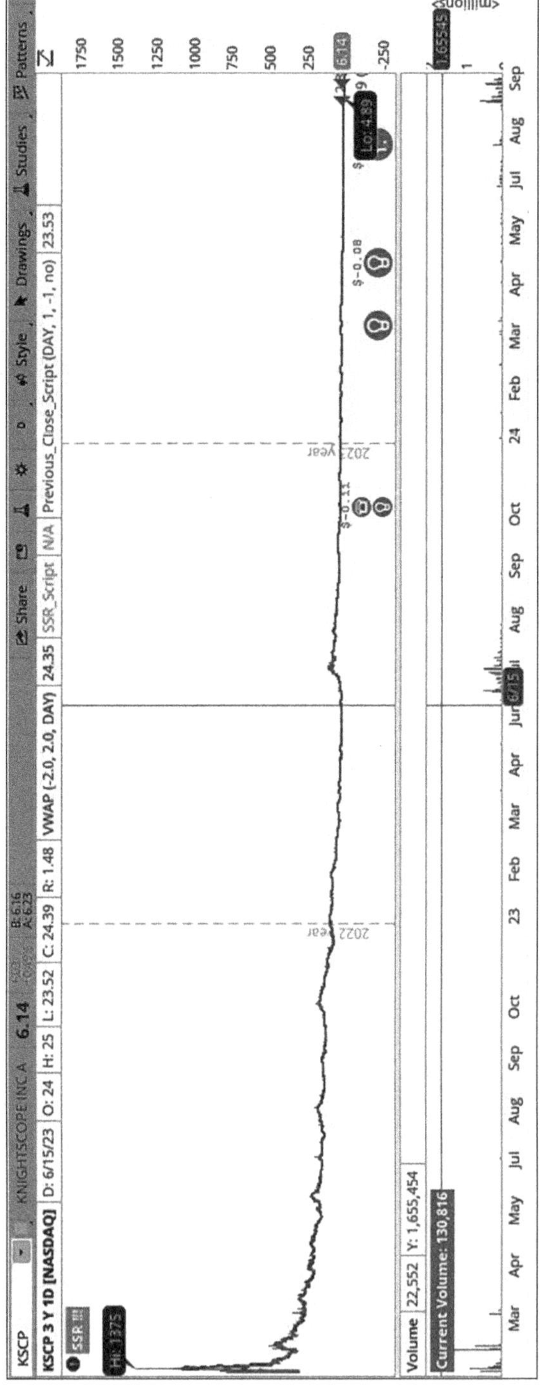

Source: Charles Schwab, thinkorswim® (TOS) software.

New York City Mayor Eric Adams, a former New York Police Department transit cop, partnered with Knightscope Inc. to implement a pilot program aimed at improving safety in the city's subway system. In September 2024 the mayor was indicted and charged with federal crimes. I began looking for a short squeeze, as the company had recently done a reverse split and the stock was at a 2.8 million float. Many of my fellow short sellers would want to enter the trade, knowing that as the stock continued to rise it would be a slam-dunk opportunity. I also knew the company's backstory. The stock experienced a sudden volatility halt to the upside after a steady uptrend spanning several days, following news of Adams' indictment. The price action signaled those short sellers had heavily concentrated their positions, leading to a squeeze. As the stock surged by 80%, reaching over $20, it became a prime A+ setup, as all the indicators aligned. During the volatility halt, I had a crucial five-minute window to verify my analysis, confirming the setup was solid. Once the halt lifted, the stock provided an ideal shorting opportunity, plummeting immediately afterward. This drop suggested that the forced short-seller exits had exhausted the buying pressure, leaving minimal momentum to push the stock higher—at least in the short term.

AVALON GLOBOCARE CORP.

Another stock that caught my attention in September 2023 was Avalon GloboCare Corp. (ALBT), a biotechnology company focused on developing cell-based therapies, precision diagnostics, and clinical laboratory services. When a company reached out to me on my podcast to do a promotion on ALBT, my first thought was, "No, this is not feasible. I'm not a pumper." I contacted Steve, my short report mentor, and told him about the communication. At the time, the stock was trading at $0.50 and since the price was too low, it became clear to me that someone wanted to dump the shares or needed liquidity to exit their positions.

Steve encouraged me to go ahead and record the video the company had asked me to do on the stock and then write a short report on it to provide evidentiary proof of its dubious nature. My reasoning was strategic: I wanted to produce 'damning evidence' of questionable operations and dubious actors. I posted the video for less than 24 hours, just to satisfy my verbal agreement with the company. They had no idea that I was a short seller and was merely seeking to abide by the deliverables. The stock was inert, immovable, and illiquid. In February 2024, on no news, it popped up in the premarket, then went down. I shorted and covered it at the open. It was illiquid for months. Then—lo and behold—on June 3, 2024, without any news, it went from $0.29 to $1.44 and then dumped within regular hours. The stock was extra-manipulated—since it surpassed $0.75, it became more susceptible to manipulation, as the exchange's halt bands tighten when a stock closes below $0.75 the day prior and then goes above it the next day.

ALBT was notorious as a pump-and-dump scheme, known for its manipulation. Thus, I had unwavering conviction about shorting the stock based on my direct knowledge of the pumpers behind it. Tight halt bands are not ideal; overall, however, the extension made for a good entry for an overnight swing short, as the tight halt bands would resume normal levels the next day. Therefore, the manipulators' tactics would not be as effective and they would most likely begin to exit their positions, causing the stock to decline and eventually dump. The stock reached a peak of $1.44 (almost a 400% move on the day) before starting to fade, eventually declining within a few days. That movement provided a prime short-selling opportunity, reinforcing my conviction to stay in the play and increase position size—what I call an ideal setup.

Figure 11: ALBT daily chart showing constant paid promotion pump and dumps

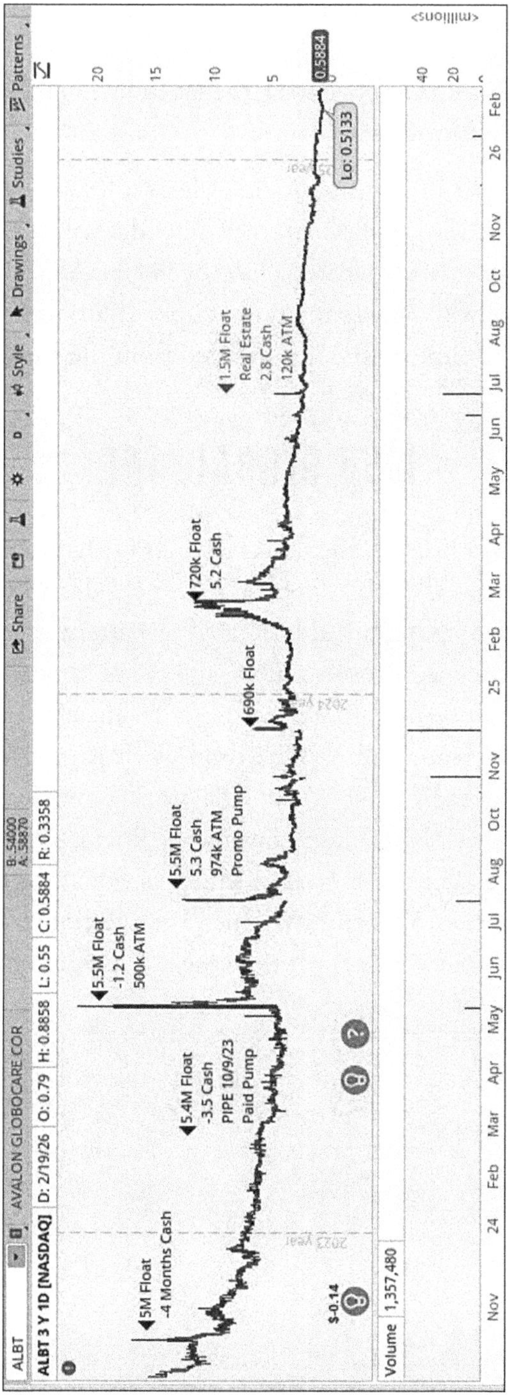

Source: Charles Schwab, thinkorswim® (TOS) software.

Then, on August 14, 2024, after a catalyst was introduced, the stock dropped sharply at 9 a.m. EST, following a massive 300% run in the premarket. By early October 2024, the stock had fallen to $0.24. Then, a reverse split cycle occurred.

Note: Once a split is completed and at least a few weeks have passed, allowing for the newly split float to be diluted, I will generally proceed to short the stock if all my criteria have been met. ALBT may continue to survive for a while using the reverse split-dilution method, but it's only a matter of time before it is delisted from the stock market.

MGO GLOBAL, INC.

Similarly, MGO Global, Inc. (MGOL) (IPO: January 2023), which has been associated with soccer star Lionel Messi, has undergone multiple reverse splits and dilutions. The pattern is clear: MGOL dilutes its stock, enacts reverse splits, and raises capital through press releases and paid promotions. This leads to an increase in supply, a decrease in demand, and a price drop, with a high probability of delisting. After each reverse split, the stock often sees brief spikes, but there can be violent squeezes when the float is very low. The ideal scenario occurs after these massive squeezes, when the company uses them as a dilution opportunity. Once the dilution takes place, the stock becomes a very easy short (like the abovementioned stocks).

Figure 12: MGOL daily chart showing reverse split pump and dump

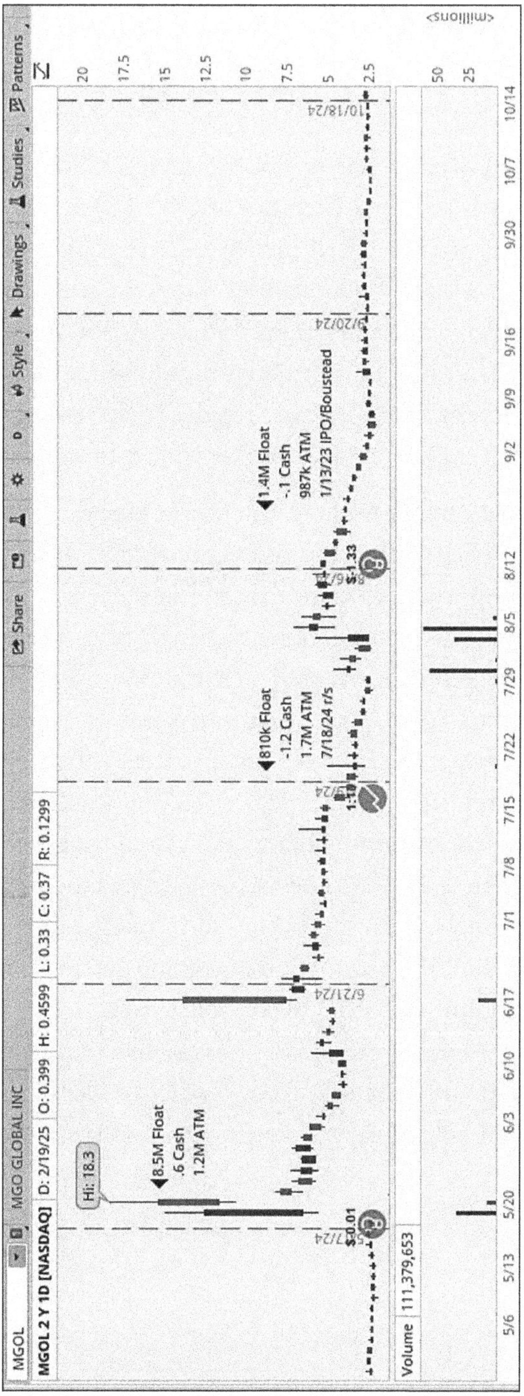

Source: Charles Schwab, thinkorswim® (TOS) software.

FARADAY FUTURE INTELLIGENT ELECTRIC, INC.

My biggest win of all time—$75,000 over several days—was trading Faraday Future Intelligent Electric, Inc. (FFIE) stock (IPO: July 22, 2021). FFIE was a U.S.-based luxury electric vehicle company with many Chinese insiders. Technically, it was not a Chinese stock, which would strictly go against my rules. However, this stock had a brick-and-mortar location in California with only some ties to China and was borderline bankrupt. I conducted a risk-reward analysis and determined that the potential reward significantly outweighed the risk.

As a discretionary trader with a high level of experience, you can make such decisions by assessing the risk-to-reward ratio and surrounding factors. It is important to note that most trades do not present the perfect scenario. You must look at the totality of the circumstances involved before entering any trade. At the time FFIE ran, I had just arrived in Buenos Aires, Argentina, and I was oblivious to its runup over three to five days. I would not have traded the stock anyway: it didn't meet my minimum entry criteria and had excessively high volume during the runup—billions of shares traded for more than three consecutive days. That level of demand was too extreme. In such situations, I wait for volume to show signs of tapering off, indicating weakness, as maintaining that kind of trading activity is unsustainable. But it was serendipitous—the stock just landed in my purview of vision, so I was able to see it from a fresh perspective and react accordingly. (Short sellers should be reactive, not predictive like long traders.) My delayed reaction helped me to have mental clarity on the trade.

A word to the wise

To be a high-level trader, you must pay attention to the surrounding conditions that affect your trade. Contrary to the prevailing belief, traveling and trading don't mix. Physical and time zone considerations (e.g., sickness and jet lag) can throw off my communication with others and my overall mental acuity and physical readiness. My own statistics show that I don't trade well when I travel. Whenever I travel, I go into retirement, so to speak, exiting only under extraordinary circumstances. I have to settle in first, and be measured and careful with every move, if I intend to be active in the market. The surrounding conditions must support my ability to trade.

By the time I traded FFIE, I had been settled in Buenos Aires for a week. I was comfortable with the ambience and suitably equipped with everything I needed for a successful trade (e.g., my computer setup and ample amounts of coffee).

On May 14, 2024, the stock traded below $1. A few days previously, it had begun a dramatic ascent, rising from $0.11 to over $5, achieving an astounding 5000% increase within a span of five to six days. No one on the trade's short-selling side could survive such a massive surge. However, I had a set threshold and did not enter the trade until the stock had surpassed $2. Up until that point, it was highly active, trading over 1 billion shares each day for multiple days. I looked for signs of a momentum shift to capture the downfall on the short side. That absurd trading volume was unsustainable—most likely fueled by market manipulation, possibly originating from China or other overseas sources. For several days, billions of shares traded with no substantial news to justify the activity. When the stock traded over 1 billion shares for three consecutive days and surged thousands of percent over a short period, I considered shorting it. The volume spike couldn't last indefinitely and was bound to exhaust, setting up an inevitable FRD opportunity.

Figure 13: FFIE daily chart showing FRD pattern

Source: Charles Schwab, thinkorswim® (TOS) software.

THESIS

- **Potential for a short squeeze**: The float was 42 million. A significant portion of these shares was gradually accumulated over approximately a week before the price surge, averaging around $0.20 per share. This accumulation was most likely orchestrated by nefarious individuals intending to execute a market manipulation scheme. This implies that acquiring most of the float could cost between $5 million and $6 million. From a market vantage point, that is not a lot of money to purchase the float and control the supply, causing a major short squeeze.
- **No news, debt, wash trading**: The combination of no news and significant debt screamed manipulation, with rogue individuals wash trading billions of shares (i.e., simultaneously buying and selling the stock to create the illusion of market activity without any actual change in ownership, designed to manipulate the appearance of market volume, prices, and demand). The company got away with its artificial trading activity because of its probable ties to overseas insiders, unchecked and outside the purview of the SEC.
- **Possible algorithm**: In addition, perhaps there was a predatory short-squeeze algorithm in wash trading at the same time.
- **Other factors**: All I knew was that the movement was not organic, the price action was unsustainable, and eventually the stock would capitulate.

METHODOLOGY

In situations presented by stocks such as FFIE, the key is to employ strategic entry criteria. When a stock trades with that much volume, the end is invariably near. In the case of FFIE, its precipitous rise from $0.11 to over $2 in just a few days was very rare. In this case, I tiptoed cautiously because of the stock's ties to China. When it surged to over 2000%, the stock went into a parabolic halt—one of my favorite plays. I sized into the trade, waited until it crashed, then played it safe and covered my position. Just when I was convinced it was done, the stock rebounded all the way up by the day's end and opened up even higher at over 5000% the next day. I re-shorted the stock on these bounces and knew it was a great judgment call. After such an unsustainable trading volume of 1 billion shares per day for multiple consecutive days, the float was updated to 439 million. In hindsight, the agenda most likely was to create an artificial, manipulated wash-trading volume, generated to dump millions of shares—a highly questionable operation.

THE FATE OF FFIE

Since my success with FFIE, the company has done several reverse splits. As long as the float remains over 2 million, its tradability depends on other factors that fall within my criteria. Since the reverse split, FFIE has traded at a few dollars and has followed a certain pattern. It fades off for a few days or a week, and the short sellers who swung it over that period begin to cover their positions. Then suddenly, the stock squeezes dramatically. When a stock hits 40% up on the day, it pops up on my scanner and I will think about shorting it—especially if no news activity accompanies it and I can read the chart clearly. For example, if the stock fades over several days, prompting short sellers who were profitable in the trade to start covering their positions to realize their gains, a short squeeze is more likely to occur. If I can clearly confirm this thesis, I will consider shorting the stock. Otherwise, I'll ignore the squeeze, as it could indicate other factors at play, potentially extending the squeeze further. My goal is to avoid being blindsided wherever possible. Then, it will fade for a short time and repeat the cycle. Today, however, FFIE (FFAI as of March 10, 2025) is at around $1.00. It is a dilution machine and eventually will find its way out. In the meantime, it is still listed on the exchanges, utilizing reverse splits to barely meet the exchanges' listing requirements. This demonstrates the lengths to which these companies will go, in most instances, to remain listed and avoid the risk of extinction.

LESSONS LEARNED FROM FFIE

FFIE illustrated the meaning of short sellers adding liquidity to the market. Short sellers covering their positions can add liquidity because when they buy back shares to close their positions, this benefits the market as a whole. Usually, there is reduced demand for the stock at lower price levels, given the typically negative factors affecting the stock's price. This act of buying to cover not only adds liquidity but can also influence stock price movements. For instance, when a stock like FFIE declines for two or three days and then surges by over 40%, this can be due to short sellers buying back shares to cover their positions, which can drive up demand and prices. This dynamic may lead to a short squeeze, where rising prices compel more short sellers to cover, fueling further upward momentum, followed by subsequent crashes and slow-bleed fades. This cycle 'rinses and repeats,' driving volatility, until the stock disappears from the market altogether.

Such a high-conviction trade as FFIE occurs only once or twice a year. Although I trade consistently, I've learned from experience to trade less frequently over the year-long period, as heightened market activity occurs in different cycles. As a short seller, it's essential first to build a financial cushion by focusing on small wins and gradually accumulating capital. This approach provides the seed money needed to take advantage of major opportunities in the future, such as that which FFIE presented. Patience and awaiting the big trades potentially can make my year in certain instances. Until then, I'm judicious and I trade what the market gives me.

A word to the wise

It's important to trade small, observe, and note every trade for the first couple of years or so, and not size up into trades like FFIE all at once. Trading with size must be learned and developed slowly and meticulously.

For example, in 2015 and 2016 respectively, I noted KaloBios Pharmaceuticals (KBIO) and shipping company Dryships (DRYS), which exhibited the patterns of pump and dumps, with huge price surges (in November 2016, DRYS soared from $1.50 to $150) and concomitant massive squeezes. I just observed these at first, without entering the trade; the risk was far too great for a novice yet to devise a proven strategy. However, after seeing these two stocks surge exponentially, I incorporated this insight into my learning process—a crucial step that enhanced my knowledge. Today, my landscape is very different. Time, patience, and education fuel impetus, build confidence, and are conducive to success.

MOMENTUS, INC.

Another great short was Momentus, Inc. (MNTS), shown in Figure 14. When the SEC declared the space-focused stock was engaged in dubious activity, this validated concerns about the company's legitimacy. This development underscored the risks associated with speculative ventures in unproven sectors. Companies like this often struggle on the stock exchange, constantly in need of cash and relying on the reputations of more established players to attract attention. They typically try to capitalize on a trending sector—space, in this case—without delivering substantial value.

Figure 14: MNTS daily chart showing dilution pump and fade over time

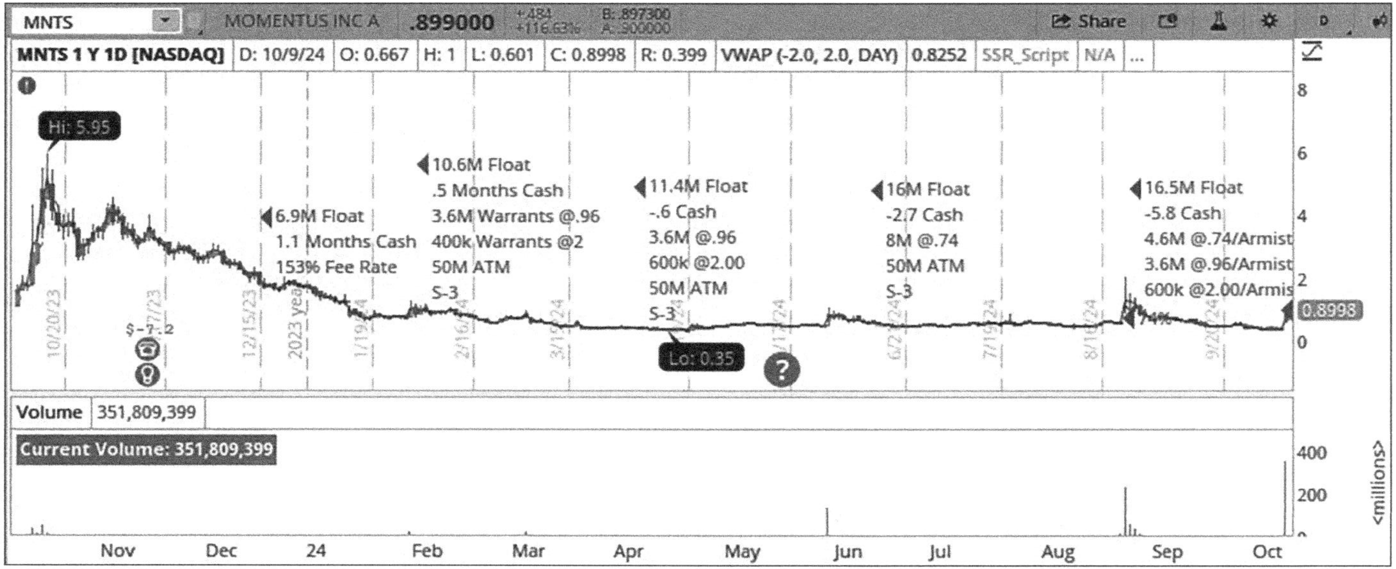

Source: Charles Schwab, thinkorswim® (TOS) software.

MNTS had concluded small deals with NASA, which generally provides modest grants to companies in the space industry. The amounts were inconsequential; but because of NASA's headline mention, a lot of hype surrounded this particular stock whenever it put out news related to NASA. Despite this limited engagement, MNTS often used this association as a promotional tool, leveraging headlines to attract investors. However, its claims lacked substantial backing.

MNTS had also touted a water-propulsion system as a unique feature, supposedly distinguishing it from competitors using traditional fuel and oxidizer methods. However, its stock followed a predictable pattern seen in pump and dumps. When the float is low, the price is pumped up; but frequent dilutions through warrants and ATM offerings increase the float significantly. This leads to inevitable downward selling pressure and the company typically resorts to a reverse stock split. After the split, the float decreases, initiating a cycle where it raises more funds, releases optimistic press statements, attracts buyers, and then the stock price inevitably falls as the dilution is unloaded.

For short sellers, it is essential to be cautious at low stock prices. Personally, I use warrant prices as an entry guide. In 2024, MNTS warrants ranged between $0.96 and $2. I consider these levels, between and above the warrant prices, ideal for shorting.

Significantly, stocks can be manipulated with less liquidity in the premarket, as there are fewer people awake and the algorithms most likely are dormant. The spread—the bid and the ask order—are further apart, so the stock can jump exponentially on light volume; essentially, it floats on thin air. Traditional stop-loss orders do not work effectively in the premarket. Therefore, the premarket can be highly susceptible to manipulation at times.

When analyzing these patterns, I pay close attention to how recent the reverse split is. While I avoid trading stocks with nano floats (under 1 million), I still monitor them, as their spikes are often short-lived, typically lasting just a day or two before dropping sharply. These stocks tend to have built-in resistance, which I term 'bag-holder resistance'—meaning long traders are reluctant to cut their losses. Many individual bag-holders fervently hold on to the hope that the stock will recover to its original price, allowing them an exit and a sigh of relief to get out at breakeven.

For example, a trader might buy a stock at $5, only to watch it fall to $4, then $3, and so on. That trader, like many others, clings to the hope that the stock will return to $5 so they can recover their losses and come out breaking even. This behavior is driven by human nature: people feel the pain of loss and long for a return to the status quo ante. Novice investors are particularly prone to this behavior and their emotional responses manifest in chart patterns. Just as one person holds the bag, it's likely that many others are similarly situated, creating resistance at the stock's prior price levels.

As long as the stock remains below that level, these bag-holders are eager to sell for breakeven as the stock price begins to approach the initial buying price, creating downward pressure on the stock whenever the stock price approaches that level. This environment, where resistance meets supply, is often ideal for short sellers, as it increases the likelihood of further declines each time the stock price nears that level, as more people hold the bag, longing to exit the trade. The best scenario for short sellers occurs when the shares of bag-holders, insiders, and warrant-holders are sold off and ATMs are added to the float, increasing supply and causing a price drop, making the stock easier to short. That is why I stick to $250 million small caps or less. This kind of movement does not occur with blue-chip stocks, which people hold on to for years.

However, if the catalyst is a medical innovation—like a breakthrough in cancer or Alzheimer's-related research—or if a billionaire purchases the stock, the crowd become engaged and excited. In that case, the stock can move way past the resistance. Generally, the bag-holders will not stay around for that rocket ride. I generally avoid trading biotech stocks because I'm not in the medical field and the news can be hard to interpret. In addition, there are many funds in the biotech space with sophisticated resources that can take up large positions in the stock's float which are inflated by algorithms. This is very tough competition, and I am extremely hesitant to participate against these stocks, which often come with a high level of speculative promise. These days, I prefer trading at the market open (9:30 a.m. EST), instead of during premarket hours. The open typically has more volume and clearer price action, while the premarket is often illiquid and volatile. I look for stocks that have moved up by over 100% on the day by the time the market opens, due to news or other catalysts. Given their desperate need for cash, these companies most likely will tap into dilution and fall back or fade.

I have encountered situations where a stock's surge exceeded 500% over multiple days, driven mostly by a short squeeze, which I always seek to avoid. To mitigate this, I look for an FRD pattern.

A confluence of factors occurs that creates a perfect storm for short sellers: a stock experiences a volatile cycle driven by a combination of profit taking, panic selling, and manipulation by large players in the market, which also sell as part of their agenda. Large investors or traders with substantial positions in the stock might decide to sell after a significant upward movement, locking in their profits. This selling can exert downward pressure on the stock price, especially if the market perceives these large exits as a signal that the stock has reached a peak. As the stock rises initially, many smaller traders and investors, motivated by FOMO, rush in to buy, chasing it upward.

This surge of buying activity can cause a further, often unsustainable, rise in price. At this stage, optimism increases and the momentum can feel unstoppable. But when the stock starts to decline, those late to the party (who bought at higher prices) begin to panic. Seeing their gains quickly erode—or, worse, facing mounting losses—many traders and investors hastily sell to cut their losses. This selling wave rapidly drives the price down, which can trigger a volatility halt that the exchange has in place. A volatility halt can occur in response to an excessive price movement and panic selling in the stock price. It typically lasts for five minutes when the price moves beyond a certain threshold, based on a predefined variable criterion set by the stock exchange. Observing the growing weakness in the stock, short sellers begin to enter the scene. Some short sellers may have already covered their positions during the stock's ascent; but now, seeing the price decline and the selling frenzy from panic-stricken long holders, new short sellers begin to pile in, sensing a profitable opportunity as the stock price crumbles.

As the stock price nears critical support levels, it may hang precariously, seemingly vulnerable to further declines. At this point, market manipulators—who may have been involved in earlier stages of the stock's rise—can take advantage of the situation.

With the stock appearing fragile and investor confidence shaken, short sellers often intensify their efforts, aggressively selling into the weakness. This creates a self-reinforcing cycle of pressure on the stock price, driving it down further. The selling accelerates as more investors capitulate, convinced that the stock's value is rapidly deteriorating.

Behind the scenes, some market manipulators may exploit these chaotic conditions to their advantage. They may have profited from the initial runup, exiting with substantial gains, and are now potentially betting on the stock's decline. Their influence can exacerbate the stock's volatility, leading to exaggerated price movements that further shake investor confidence.

In some cases, if the stock reaches a particularly low level, either it might experience a final wave of capitulation—where even the most steadfast investors sell in despair—or, if the short selling becomes overextended, a short squeeze may occur, causing the stock to be temporarily overextended. This leads to a 'bounce short' play. This happens when short sellers are forced to cover their positions as the stock rebounds sharply, driven by either value investors stepping in or unexpected positive news occurring in combination with short sellers covering. Such reversals are erratic, with the stock price recovering dramatically in a short period.

Given my keen awareness of these price movements, I am meticulous about my practices, which include daily journaling and daily YouTube stock trading reviews, which I broadcast to subscribers to *The Friendly Bear*. I use the YouTube channel as my personal archive of each stock I trade—a treasure trove of information. I go the extra mile to examine and analyze the institutional ownership and the stock's commonalities, losses, and wins to discover why people buy a particular stock and why they don't sell. I pay particular attention to possible scenarios in which people will be averse to selling. During the pandemic, people termed this a 'diamond hands' scenario—a trend that has since largely disappeared but that can resurface when certain news headlines capture investors' imagination. They will then 'lock hands' and refrain from selling immediately.

Even if a trade is green, I will seek to discover what I did right and what I could potentially have missed. I also maintain a highly organized video archive that documents the stock's history—past, present, and future—including ticker symbols. I review my own videos at 2.0 speed after recording them. Like a pro athlete who studies their taped plays, I analyze the synopsis of each stock. This serves as a memory refresher and helps sustain my trading performance.

We discretionary traders are like sage conductors, overseeing a symphony with precision, knowing exactly when to intervene—especially when considering and analyzing those stocks that lack fundamental strength and legitimacy and appear poised to fall. The short seller's success is contingent on an ability to recognize the subtle cues and patterns that signal inevitable decline—all while maintaining intense focus, mental acuity, and calmness. My mental exercises and vitamin intake fuel my ability to 'conduct' this symphony and achieve my desired outcome amid the proliferation of emotional activity.

THE DUBIOUS STOCK PATTERN

To recap—dubious stocks have telltale stories and trajectories:

- The stock has little to no institutional ownership—the less the better. Five percent ownership or less is ideal for a clean short.
- The company has a dubious reputation.
- The company lacks substance and utility.
- The stock is up 40% or more on the day.
- The company has a significant cash need (with just three months or less of cash left).
- The company has changed its stock ticker symbol.
- The company has a history of repeatedly diluting its stock.
- The company has a history of issuing many warrants.

The above rules encapsulate my three-dimensional thesis about stocks. I don't simply follow patterns. I have an architect's view of the world, such that I intuitively visualize how the lines and shapes of candlestick patterns translate into actual spatial forms or trades. This involves a *mental rotation* of objects, understanding volume, scale, how spaces relate to one another, and the outcome of the 'design'—hopefully, well-thought-out strategies that translate into a successful trade.

A stock's story and the people behind it tell me how to depict an outcome visually whether the stock will move up or down—depending on its inherent purpose and the goals behind it, if any. This knowledge translates into short-selling success with astounding accuracy.

Traders don't need to navigate the entire market to find profitable opportunities. By focusing on the abovementioned stocks and others like them, and by carefully timing entries around key warrant levels, they potentially can achieve consistent returns through judicious shorting at just the right moment.

As a discretionary trader, I liken myself to a cheetah—an apex predator with remarkable speed and strength. The cheetah preys on weaker or compromised animals, resulting in a high efficiency or win rate, rather than expending energy on larger, potentially dangerous prey that could cause them harm.

This analogy is closely aligned with my approach to trading. I am highly selective in choosing my trades, focusing on stocks with market caps of $250 million or less, often from highly speculative and borderline dubious activity. These are typically shell companies, operating without a real address or out of a makeshift office (e.g., a shed). The CEOs often have a history of dubious activities, and the companies perpetually need to raise capital, relying on the same predatory lenders that extract their gains by giving them the money they need to survive for a deep discount on their current stock price. In essence, the company is selling its soul for survival. These lenders acquire shares at low cost and proceed to dump them. As described in Chapter 10 and in the above discussion on companies that engage in reverse splits, the cycle then repeats continuously. Such is the nature of shorts, upon which we cheetahs capitalize.

A word to the wise

Trader-speak—lingo grounded in uncertainty

Due to the market's inherent unpredictability, we traders never speak in certainties. Instead, we articulate our thoughts and opinions in probabilities, odds, and likelihoods (i.e., 'It's more or less likely a company will ...' or 'It's highly probable that the company will do X in the future/will trade in Y way'). In the world of trading, certainty and declarative sentences are dangerous and can wreak havoc (e.g., short squeezes). One word can change everything, and we must be careful to avoid assumptions, emotional reactions, or hasty conclusions about anything. Variabilities are essential to short-selling dynamics because of diverse factors, including volatility, price fluctuations, unexpected world events, market reactions, and behavioral factors.

Easy money strategies

It's important, when starting out on your trading journey, to have one simple, easy-money strategy that makes you feel confident about the stocks you trade. I have a basket of stocks that I always depend on whenever they make a significant move. I know everything about those companies: their products, their financials, the individuals involved. I conduct extensive research that allows me to capitalize on these small-cap stocks as I learn. I short these perpetual pump-and-dump/questionable operations every time they pop up. You don't want to oversize, as these stocks can squeeze—at times, more than you'd imagine was possible. However, they are relatively safe and very select; but trading solely these stocks can yield comfortable outcomes. You should develop your own basket of such stocks. Pay attention to the telltale pump-and-dump characteristics mentioned and you will stay on course.

LESSONS LEARNED

RISK MANAGEMENT AND GRADUAL GROWTH

Starting small and gradually scaling up is essential for long-term success. The examples of FFIE, MGOL, and MNTS highlight the potential risks of trading highly volatile stocks. Careful sizing, coupled with a strong financial cushion, ensures traders can weather unexpected outcomes and seize high-conviction opportunities when they arise.

CURATING A SELECT 'BASKET' OF STOCKS

A curated watch list of familiar stocks enables consistent returns and reduces unnecessary complexity. Understanding these stocks' behaviors, key levels, and historical patterns fosters confidence and precision in trades.

AVOIDING CERTAINTY IN TRADING LANGUAGE

Traders must operate within a framework of probabilities rather than absolutes. This mindset accommodates market fluctuations, mitigating emotional responses to unexpected events. Adopting cautious, flexible language reflects a disciplined approach, helping traders remain grounded and objective.

ADOPTING A SELECTIVE APPROACH

The defining attribute of professional traders is judicious stock selection. Have a clean trading diet and be selective about the stocks you trade. By doing so and focusing on prepared setups, you avoid potential outliers. For example, by not trading nano floats (stocks under 1 million float), I have less to trade, but I am free of the danger of potential disaster. More trades do not equate to more profit.

THE CYCLICAL NATURE OF MARKETS

Market opportunities often follow predictable cycles, influenced by behavioral and structural factors. Recognizing these cycles and aligning trading strategies accordingly, as shown in the recurring patterns of stocks like ALBT and MNTS, help traders achieve consistent profitability.

TIPS AND TRICKS

- The FRD strategy is a trading approach that capitalizes on the reversal of a stock after several consecutive days of price increases, typically three to five 'green days.' During this upward trend, the stock may experience a 'blow-off top'—an unsustainable, exponential rise which is often unsupported by significant news or developments.
- A capitulation occurs when, for example, the stock price surges and many short sellers enter the market, betting that the stock is overvalued and poised for a decline. If too many short sellers pile in, this can lead to a massive short squeeze, where they are forced to buy back shares to cover their positions as the price continues to rise, inadvertently driving the price even higher. This creates maximum pressure and often results in a gap-up at the market open, further inflating the stock price.
- The FRD occurs when this upward momentum reverses, marking the first day the stock closes lower ('red') after the series of gains over the course of three to five days. This is the optimal point for traders to initiate short positions. Identifying this moment requires diligent technical analysis, meticulous journaling, and close observation of market patterns. The reversal can happen across various time frames, so being attuned to real-time market dynamics is crucial.
- A+ FRD setups—those offering the most favorable trading conditions—may occur only four to five times a year. Successfully capitalizing on these opportunities demands extensive experience, continuous market engagement, concentration, and thorough preparation. The strategy does not produce immediate success without significant practice and understanding, much like the rigorous training that an Olympic athlete puts in for a pivotal but fleeting event.

Chapter 11
OF BEARS AND BULLS

IN THIS CHAPTER, I discuss the coexistence of short sellers and long traders and how, in ideal circumstances, both can capitalize on market inefficiencies. Sophisticated traders, both long and short, usually trade at the same levels. When the long trader sells, the short enters, and vice versa. The crowd of unsophisticated traders creates inefficiencies which, in turn, are opportunities for both to capitalize. Therefore, knowledge and education—such as those provided in this book—are the cornerstones to successful participation in the market, which should be a natural yin-yang engagement without obstructing yourself or anyone else. Sophistication does not necessarily involve professional knowhow or Ivy League university training. Instead, knowledge can be gleaned organically through self-discipline and diligent study.

MUTUAL COEXISTENCE

As a seven-figure short seller with a 90%-plus win ratio, verified by *Business Insider* eight times to date, I believe that aspiring and professional traders achieve 'the win' not through rivalry and adversarial competition, but through mutual coexistence. I often analogize the relationship between short sellers and long traders to the comic superhero The Flash and his nemesis, Reverse Flash. This dynamic relationship creates a tug of war between a long trader (someone who buys, expecting the price to rise) and a short seller (someone who sells, expecting the price to fall), where neither gains the upper hand for long. However, when a long trader and a short seller work in sync, they create a more stable environment, passing the baton back and forth, aligning their actions with market cycles. This interplay ensures that prices don't spiral out of control. 'Passing the baton' speaks to timing. If both traders execute the trades at precisely the right time, they establish equilibrium: when synchronized, these conflicting forces can naturally drive toward market stability.

Ideally, the relationship between long traders and short sellers is like a coordinated, though often unconscious, relay race. To be a successful short seller, you must understand the mindset of the long trader. This requires imagining where the long positions are and predicting when profitable long traders are likely to sell those long positions.

I avoid shorting stocks in the areas where skilled long traders buy, as their buying momentum could push the stock price higher. The ideal moment for the short seller is when the long trader is ready to exit. The long trader essentially 'passes the baton' to the short seller by selling along with the short seller. At that point, both parties operate on a shared understanding of the stock's trajectory—one exiting a profitable long position, the other capitalizing on the stock's reversal. The transition from long to short can cause the stock to come back down smoothly, as one trader exits long while the other enters short. Despite their lack of knowledge about each other's actions, they are both fluent in the same language, effortlessly and unintentionally coordinating without hindering each other's strategies or getting in each other's way.

CONFLICTING INTERESTS/ ACTION VERSUS REACTION

For instance, if a nano float (a share float under 1 million) pops up on my radar, I avoid it like the plague. In contrast, a long trader could see it as a long opportunity. This is good for that individual, as I will be out of their way as a short seller. While the long trader can ride the price movements of the nano float to the upside, I, as a profitable short seller, can sit back, sip my coffee, and watch. However, if an inexperienced short seller jumps in and shorts the nano float stock, the long trader gains the odds in their favor against short sellers, as the entry of even a few short sellers increases the risk of a heightened, exponential outlier squeeze. The short seller faces a squeeze while the long trader reaps the profits.

If the stock does not have a nano float and a long trader buys shares based on good news, knowing that the company needs cash and has filed a registered Form S-3 (a 'shelf registration,' which enables companies to register securities in advance and sell them later 'off the shelf' when market conditions become favorable), and can issue an offering at any moment—or, alternatively, that unlocked shares can be sold into the stock's float, diluting it by increasing the supply—the long trader should ideally act quickly to capitalize on the stock's upward move. Afterwards, a short seller may look to enter the market and short the stock. In this process, both the short seller and the long trader aim to capitalize on price movements, albeit at different points in time: the long trader acts before the price rises, while the short seller steps in after. Short sellers are more reactive, while long traders must be prognosticators of price movements and plan accordingly before entering a trade. Thus, both traders plan before entering, but short sellers likely are more reactive. In the small-cap space, the company needing cash will usually take advantage of upward stock movements based on hyperbolic headlines and use this opportunity to raise cash and dilute the stock if it has a registered 'shelf,' an ATM, and warrant holders seeking to cash in on their warrants. For these reasons, short selling is a high-probability strategy. So, we short sellers must manage our positions. The stock could squeeze more than we think. As the risk is inherently higher, due to the potential for prices to theoretically rise infinitely compared to the finite limit of falling to zero for long traders, this is where proper risk management and careful stock selection become critical.

While long trading is a lower-odds endeavor, there is significant opportunity in the ability to read technical patterns, project stock movements, spot the signs indicating demand, and ride the upward price movement waves.

For example, a company has enough cash to operate for five months. As a short seller, I look for three months of cash, ideally. While five months' cash is not a healthy amount for the company, it's not critically low either. The longs (i.e., those betting on the stock rising) are aware that the company isn't in great shape and doesn't have a lot of cash, but they also know it isn't on the verge of bankruptcy. Profitable long traders in the small-cap space are meticulous in their approach. They understand that even when a stock moves in their favor, the opportunity is often fleeting. The window to capitalize on these movements is narrow, requiring precision and decisiveness. This is precisely why I choose to focus on small caps. I clearly understand the endgame for these companies. Unlike large caps or blue-chip stocks, these are not fundamentally strong or stable businesses built for the long term. They are not household names or industry stalwarts, but their volatility creates unique opportunities for those who know how to navigate this space effectively.

FINDING YOUR LANE

The shorts understand that although the company is weak, the longs might still actively trade the stock. If there isn't significant dilution (e.g., issuing more shares), the stock price could still rise considerably by 50–100% (a conservative estimate—I have even seen low float runners go over 1000% at times if the supply is low enough), which would be painful for those shorting it. Meanwhile, the longs know that if the shorts enter too early at a low price and the stock starts to rise, the shorts could get squeezed, forcing them to cover their positions—which could drive the price even higher, allowing the longs to profit.

In this scenario, a combination of inexperienced, undisciplined, and less knowledgeable traders might get in each other's way, making poor, emotional decisions that cause them to overlap. But skilled and profitable traders will take advantage of these dynamics, capitalizing on the opportunities created by both the shorts and the longs.

THE SIGNIFICANCE OF A METICULOUS RISK MANAGEMENT PROCESS

To trade successfully (with either short selling or long trading), effective risk management and precise timing are key. Whether you're a short seller or a long trader, you can't simply enter a trade at any moment. For example, when dealing with a stock that has a nano float and high institutional ownership, blindly entering the trade creates a substantial risk on the short side. Traders on both the long side and the short side must undertake a meticulous, unassailable process before entering a trade, analogous to a pilot's preflight checklist. You must know when to enter, when to exit, and how much you're willing to risk.

DIFFERENT STROKES—THE PERFECT STORM FOR BULLS AND BEARS

When long traders search for the perfect setup, they strive for the convergence of two or three crucial factors that create an ideal scenario—a 'perfect storm' for a long position which significantly improves their odds of success. This process is not an exact science. For example, if a company has a higher percentage of institutional ownership and the float is very low, this sets the stage for a possible long position if a confluence of factors aligns positive news, strong earnings, and broader market trends favoring the stock. If there is no dilution and the stock has a small float with significant insider ownership, it is typically a strong candidate for a potential long position—particularly if a compelling headline emerges or the relevant sector experiences a sudden surge in interest.

The volatility and high demand create favorable conditions for long traders. As long as demand and volume remain strong, this environment benefits the longs. However, as demand tapers off, the short seller gains the advantage. In many instances, when news initially surfaces in the small-cap arena, volume and demand are strong and favor long traders, who can capitalize; but they must be aware of the unsustainable nature of this volume/demand, which will eventually taper off when the price surges and the stock begins its reverse trend.

VWAP AND SHORT SELLER BEHAVIOR

In the premarket open, short sellers often cover their positions below the VWAP. Before covering, a catalyst may trigger a surge, leading to increased buying pressure. As short sellers begin closing their positions, the VWAP acts as a resistance level due to the concentrated selling activity in that area.

A squeeze forms around the VWAP as short sellers exit to lock in profits, causing the price to temporarily rise before pulling back. Once the stock breaks below the VWAP, it confirms the reversal, making this an ideal area to cover. However, caution is necessary: stocks can float back up and trigger another breakout later in the day.

The VWAP functions like a water mark: trading above it is like being above water, while trading below it is like being underwater.

SCREEN TIME AND CANDLE SELECTION IN TRADING

Screen time is crucial for anyone learning to trade. I primarily use the one-minute candle for intraday trading but frequently switch between the one-minute and five-minute candles. Often, the five-minute candles provide a clearer read on market direction. The one-minute chart can be noisy, with rapid green spikes that can mislead beginners and intermediate traders into expecting a reversal that never comes.

THE IMPORTANCE OF FIVE-MINUTE CANDLES

Algorithms and institutional traders often rely on five-minute candles because they provide a more reliable indication of stock direction. If the five-minute candle closes red, it often signals a stronger trend. However, I prefer trading off the one-minute chart for its volatility—it provides better insight into real-time volume, which aligns with Level 2 data and time and sales (see Chapter 8 for a full explanation of my process), rather than waiting for the five-minute candle to close.

CHARTING STRATEGY

LOOK 10-15 DAYS OUT

Key questions to ask include the following:

- Are we seeing continuation from a previous runup?

- Did the stock have news five days ago that could lead to covering now?
- Is there a liquidity trap? A liquidity trap happens when a stock experiences an unexpected green day—whether due to news, algorithms, or even no news at all—triggering a short squeeze and sending the price surging by hundreds of percentage points. When too many short sellers are caught in the stock, small caps present significant opportunities but also extreme risks, especially for short sellers.
- If a stock trades 100 million shares one day but drops to just 3 million the next, ask yourself the following questions:
  - How much of that volume was algorithmic or wash trading?
  - If 50 million shares were algo-driven, the other 50 million shares were real participants who still need to exit—who is left to cover?

A liquidity trap results in traders being stuck with no easy exit, wider spreads, and a domino effect if a major player ignites a move.

BE CAUTIOUS OF FIRST GREEN DAYS WITH HIGH VOLUME

If a stock has a massive volume day but lacks exit volume for short sellers or other traders, it can create a dangerous setup. Always consider the broader context before shorting the first green day.

THE BIGGER PICTURE: MULTI-YEAR CHARTS

Zoom out beyond the intraday chart. Switch between one-year and five-year (or even multi-year) charts. Many small-cap stocks trend downward over time, indicating weak companies. Ask yourself the following questions:

- Are we at yearly lows, signaling a potential bottom bounce?
- Is there a hard bounce that could trigger short covering and crowding?

Don't get trapped in an overly narrow intraday focus—it's a dead end. While small caps provide excellent opportunities, always step back to see the overall trend and market context.

ANCHORED VWAP: FACILITATOR OF MARKET BEHAVIOR ANALYSIS

When analyzing price movements, I exclusively use an anchored VWAP (AVWAP), as indicated in Figure 15. This method offers us short sellers X-ray-like vision to analyze price movements and pick better entries on the short side. I prefer to anchor the VWAP from the prior day's close, using the top deviation as a resistance level. This approach helps identify cleaner short entry opportunities. That is, the AVWAP allows traders to analyze price action in a more precise and flexible manner by anchoring the calculation to specific time points, such as important events, price pivots, or trend reversals. The ability to adapt makes it more efficient than the regular VWAP, which is calculated over a fixed period, like a single trading day, and resets at the start of each new session. While the traditional VWAP calculates the average price over a predetermined time frame, the AVWAP offers the flexibility to adjust it to any significant point chosen by the trader. This feature provides a more tailored and pertinent understanding of market behavior and helps traders identify more meaningful support and resistance levels, assess the impact of specific market events, and make better-informed decisions—all of which are limited by the static nature of the regular VWAP.

Figure 15: REVB 1-minute chart showing entry level at top deviation of AVWAP near 10 a.m. EST

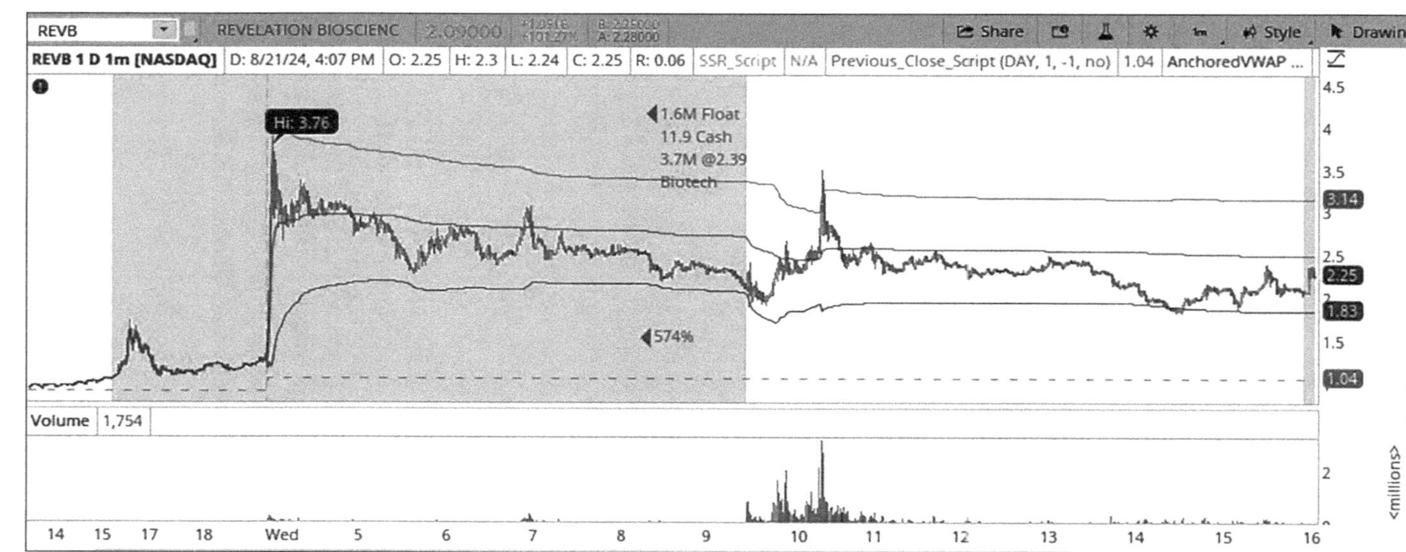

Source: Charles Schwab, thinkorswim® (TOS) software.

The AVWAP chart is a useful tool for traders to determine the average stock price at which stock traders have entered the market. The chart's salient characteristic is its ability to let traders select a specific starting point, or 'anchor,' which is beneficial for analyzing price movements following significant events such as a company's earnings report, a substantial price increase, or a market downturn.

VWAP LINE

The 'average price' is determined by considering the quantity of shares purchased at various prices. The price of a certain stock is more influential if many shares have been bought at that price.

The VWAP line serves as a reference point to determine whether the current price is higher or lower than the average price paid by individuals since a specific starting point, such as a major news event.

DEVIATIONS

These are like 'bands' or zones that show how far the price has moved away from the VWAP:

- **Upper deviation:** Shows that the price is much higher than the average. This could mean the stock is extended or overbought.
- **Lower deviation:** Shows that the price is much lower than the average. This could mean the stock has found a bottom or oversold.

WHEN DOES THIS HELP?

Let's say you're looking at the stock price after an earnings report. You anchor the VWAP to that date to see the average price since then. As the stock price moves up and down, you compare it to the VWAP line and the deviations above and below.

If the stock price is well above the upper deviation, it means people are paying much more than the average price since the earnings report. This could mean it is overvalued, and the price will likely reverse to the mean (VWAP).

If the stock price is around or below the lower deviation, it could be a signal the stock is undervalued or oversold, signifying a likely influx of buying around this area, pushing the price up.

WHEN DO SHORT SELLERS BENEFIT?

Short sellers make money when the stock price drops. The AVWAP helps us spot moments when the price is too high or too low (especially near the top deviation) compared to what most people paid.

When the price is near or above the upper deviation, this might indicate that the stock is overvalued or overextended at the moment, and there is a higher probability to go short on it, since it is likely to have a reversal due to the significant vertical separation from the average price.

When the price drops from the upper deviation (VWAP), this is often a sign that the stock's rise is slowing or reversing, which short sellers can use as a signal to remain short or add to their position in accordance with the price action's trend. Enter the short seller.

WHEN DO LONG TRADERS BENEFIT?

As the price moves toward the upper deviation, long traders may consider taking profits, expecting a possible retracement (a brief pause or pullback in an upward or downward movement).

A retrace to the middle deviation (VWAP) could offer a re-entry opportunity or a chance to add to an existing long position, as it suggests the price is stabilizing around the average value. If the price consolidates in this area for an extended period and holds at or above the VWAP, this indicates bullish price action. As the trading day approaches the final hour, this setup may position the stock for a breakout, potentially triggering a short squeeze that could amplify the breakout's momentum. Coupled with existing news or a catalyst, the move could escalate into an outlier 'power hour' squeeze. This kind of scenario is crucial for short sellers to avoid and equally important for long traders to recognize, as they can capitalize on the opportunity.

A drop in price to the bottom deviation could signal a buying opportunity for long traders and a cover opportunity for short sellers—although the price drop could be temporary. This could lead to an upward bounce to the nearest resistance level, since the stock was oversold at the lower AVWAP deviation. The security has higher bounce-back odds due to the long traders' 'dip buying,' along with the short sellers' buy-to-cover purchase of shares. This is particularly true if other indicators or price actions indicate oversold conditions (e.g., if the stock price finds key support levels from longer time frames).

Short sellers and long traders have a mutual understanding. For instance, if I short a stock at the upper deviation and ideally look to exit or cover my position at a lower point, I must buy back the shares. My action hypothetically passes the baton to the longs, who may look to buy at the lower deviation. In that case, we buy at the same level, using different methods that result in the same outcome—buying. Shorts buy to cover; longs buy outright. Both forms of buying are representative of demand, which pushes the price up for that moment. This can be reflected through Level 2 Time and Sales (which displays a time log of executed trades and each completed transaction). If the long trader buys at the lower deviation, the short seller ideally avoids entering as the price is already oversold, having dropped to the AVWAP's lower deviation.

A word to the wise

I don't chase weak and declining stocks on the short side. That is analogous to a situation in which long traders with FOMO chase ascending stock. I seek to short extended stocks or short on strength after the stock has dropped from its initial run. Ideally, the strength is temporary and heading into upcoming resistance levels—the best time for initiating my short position. I can foresee such an opportunity from looking at the charts.

Later, if the long trader sells around the upper deviation to lock in profit, the short seller might seek to enter. At this point, both traders sell together without conflict, operating concurrently.

The traders who are not aligned are those who are unaware of AVWAP and use only VWAP to understand when the long traders seek to buy and the shorts look to cover. That is when things become complicated. For example, the shorts might short at the lower deviation, which is too early, putting them at odds with the longs—in a place where the long traders look to buy. This positions them to face a potential squeeze—a scenario where demand will most likely arise and push the stock up. The goal of the long traders is to sell on the upper deviation of AVWAP; and if shorts enter prematurely, they position themselves at higher odds to encounter a squeeze and might seek to cut their losses. Basically, the ideal goal of the long traders is to buy at the lower deviation and sell at the upper deviation.

BEWARE OF THE SHORT SQUEEZE

As a short seller, I must be careful of stocks that consolidate around the VWAP for a few hours or more, as that indicates a potential squeeze, which I seek to avoid. This sideways price action or consolidation, combined with steady volume throughout the day, often signals a tug-of-war between long traders and short sellers. When demand increases and short sellers experience overcrowding, the stock can break out, potentially triggering exponential short squeezes—which are more prone to happen at the last hour of the trading day, or 'power hour.' At that time, if a stock consolidates around or above the VWAP with steady volume, long traders frequently buy into stocks holding near their highs, with a momentum that often drives breakouts to new highs. When short sellers accumulate in a stock and buyers start to step in, a rising price—especially in the final trading hour—can act as a catalyst for a breakout. This upward momentum may trigger a short squeeze, driving accelerated buying pressure and resulting in parabolic price action.

As buying intensifies, short sellers are forced to cover their positions, triggering a chain reaction of stop-outs. This domino effect drives prices higher, especially when the stock has limited supply and significant demand.

DEGREES OF EXTENSION BEYOND THE VWAP

Again, the VWAP reflects the average price from a specific point and the further the stock moves away from it, the greater the likelihood it will revert to the mean, represented by the lower weighted average. This indicator helps me to assess better entries and exits. It is important to note, however, that the AVWAP strategy is an indicator and more like an art of pattern recognition, not an exact science.

If the stock rises above the VWAP parabolically, it will likely be extended and I will seek to short it if it meets my strict criteria. That's why I prefer using the AVWAP—because it assists in identifying when a stock is overextended at the current prices, including the upper and lower deviations—in addition to VWAP, which helps identify the overextension. When the price reaches the upper deviation, it indicates that the stock has significantly extended and is likely to face resistance, potentially pulling back toward the VWAP.

ACTIVE SELLING—A PRIME LANDSCAPE FOR THE SHORT SELLER

I look for a clear indication of active selling, confirmed by both price action and volume. Specifically, after a stock makes an upward move and reaches the top deviation of the AVWAP, I want to observe a rejection at that level. A red candle should accompany that rejection, which has a longer body than the previous group of candles, signaling strong selling pressure. The red sell candle must close with a convincingly red, clear body, indicating heavy liquidation. Simultaneously, volume should show a noticeable shift—from steady demand to an increase in selling—which could be due to sizable long traders claiming their profits, panic selling, dilution dumping, or a combination of these. I avoid entering a short when I observe too many green candles in a row, signaling strength and a possible continuing upward trend in the stock.

A RECAPITULATION OF MY CRITERIA

The framework for long traders potentially initiating their positions might begin by identifying the inverse criteria I employ as a short seller. To reiterate, these are:

- avoidance of high institutional ownership;
- avoidance of nano floats;
- avoidance of billionaire plays (i.e., billionaires involved in the company's catalyst or headline); and
- avoidance of legitimate good news that inspires genuine excitement (e.g., biotech stocks that could promote medical advancements to the benefit of society, such as treatments for Alzheimer's or cancer, capable of capturing the human imagination and galvanizing interest).

A TALE OF TWO STOCKS: SERV AND NVIDIA

Stocks that challenge short sellers often provide an advantage to long traders. Serve Robotics Inc. (SERV), a company specializing in self-driving robotic carts (commonly described as 'little coolers on wheels'), emerged as 'a good long' in mid-2024, benefiting from a confluence of favorable factors. From my observations, the product initially encountered skepticism, mainly due to concerns over potential vandalism. However, more recent developments shifted the outlook significantly. A Form 13G filing revealed that NVIDIA and Uber had acquired a stake of 5% or higher in SERV. Their participation legitimized SERV, as NVIDIA—renowned for its dominance in computer chips and AI technology—was one of the hottest stocks in the market at the time. Uber, an autonomous ride-share service, could potentially use SERV to expand its service. The companies' interest thus indicated that SERV's technology could be strongly linked to advancements in robotics, AI, and potentially autonomous systems, powered by NVIDIA's chips.

Over a span of two and a half weeks, SERV's stock price increased from $2 to $24 and then declined again. The spike was the result of a short squeeze. Short sellers in this scenario acted as jet fuel for the short squeeze. When short sellers overcrowd a position, it creates a precarious situation in which even a small catalyst can trigger a domino effect of forced covering that can occur over several days, adding to the stock's upward momentum. To compound these circumstances, when a major catalyst—such as a top-tier company's reveal of a significant 5%+ stake in the stock—emerges, this provides a compelling reason for traders, investors, and institutions to buy. The influx of genuine demand drives the stock price higher, compelling shorts to cover their positions. Each short squeezed out further elevates the price, reinforcing the stock's ascent, which is why the jet fuel metaphor is appropriate.

Figure 16: SERV daily chart showing bullish run after NVDA ownership revealed

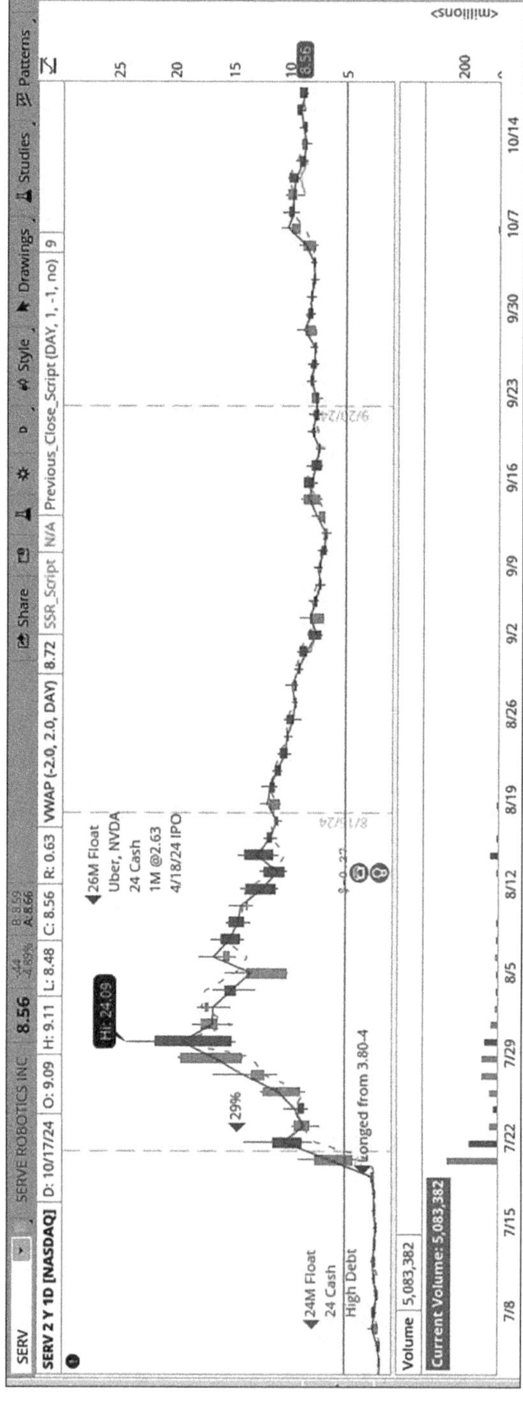

Source: Charles Schwab, thinkorswim® (TOS) software.

Since the company has minimal to no dilution overhead and no cash need, there is limited resistance at the higher levels as the stock breaks out to new highs. This dynamic causes more short sellers to cover their positions, further fueling the upward momentum and adding 'jet fuel' to the fire.

THE BENEFITS AND PITFALLS OF SHORT SELLING

As in life, there are advantages and disadvantages to short selling. You just have to understand the landscape in which you operate and be adept at fundamental and technical analysis. Stocks that do not present prime short-selling opportunities based on my strict criteria may conversely be good for going long and vice versa. The small-cap space is ideal for shorts, since we understand the endgame of these mostly bad or borderline-questionable operations in need of cash to survive; while the big-caps benefit those who seek to invest.

SHORT SELLER EXPENDITURES AND THE RISK/REWARD RATIO REQUIREMENT

Short selling involves various fees. The borrow fee rates for holding a stock overnight have increased exponentially (most recently, in May 2024). Many small-cap companies will become insolvent in the long term, but a short seller cannot hold the stock for a protracted period due to the extreme borrow fee rates.

The locate fee is an additional cost for short sellers, which can typically range from $20 to over $1,000 just for the opportunity to short, depending on how many shares they intend to locate for that purpose. Therefore, given the high borrow fee rates and the locate fees, I must have a steadfast conviction about the stocks I short. The risk/reward ratio must be around 3:1 or greater—the potential profit must outweigh the risk. Finally, short sellers must pay a small commission, which can add up quickly and eat up your profits. Finally, I pay a specialty broker platform fee of around $200 a month to receive the most efficient executions.

A word to the wise

In some instances, short sellers have a bad reputation. However, I seek to demonstrate, in all my transactions, that my primary objective is to fulfill my responsibilities without competing with others. I acknowledge that both bullish and bearish trends can exist in the market, and we all share ownership of the landscape. It's important that we are considerate and respectful of one another, as well as appreciating the benefits of achieving and maintaining balance and enlightenment. *The Friendly Bear* podcast accomplishes exactly that. My goal is to educate people about short selling by leveraging the expertise of experienced traders and exposing dubious activity of companies and dishonest individuals through YouTube videos. For instance, I exposed FLGC by personally visiting the company's headquarters in Colombia. Naturally, there were naysayers and detractors; but the visuals, along with the short report, were undeniable.

LONG TRADER FEES

To engage in long trades, traders need only a commission-free broker. Some brokers, however, are not direct access brokers. Payment for order flow is a primary way in which brokerages make money from commission-free trades. This may result in lower-quality order execution, leading to slightly higher buy prices and marginally lower sell prices, and generally disadvantageous executions for clients.

SHORT SELLER SCAPEGOATING

As for me, I simply go with the odds in my favor and stick to my process, while remaining keenly aware of the misconceptions voiced in the industry: namely, that short sellers drive down stock prices—a blatant untruth. Often, a company will attempt to scapegoat short sellers to divert attention from its dubious or failing status. For example, in early 2023, global edtech company Genius Group Limited (GNS) released press statements to promote itself as a catalyst for change and declared it had hired a former Federal Bureau of Investigation director to investigate alleged naked short selling of its stock—announcements which attracted buyers to pump the stock.

A word to the wise

The illegal practice of 'naked short selling' manipulates and destabilizes the market by attempting to sell shares that the short seller may not own or has merely borrowed. This can drive down the stock price unfairly and create instability through the trading of stocks that may not actually exist. Some companies try to capitalize on naked short selling by imputing this wrongdoing to short sellers to divert attention from their own speciousness.

In the case of GNS, the stock experienced a temporary upswing as investors became enthusiastic. But this was artificial manipulation, most likely intended to further the company's agenda to take advantage of the higher price to raise cash through offerings or other means. From January through May 2023, the stock saw a 1500% rise, only to plummet and fade 1500%. This was not due to the shorts; instead, multiple offerings over time increased the float, which caused downward pressure on the stock and its collapse to its true value.

LESSONS LEARNED

MUTUAL COEXISTENCE BENEFITS THE MARKET

Collaboration and respect between long traders and short sellers create a balanced and efficient market. By synchronizing their actions, traders help stabilize stock prices and mitigate volatility, benefiting the overall trading ecosystem.

TIMING AND RISK MANAGEMENT ARE CRUCIAL

Both long traders and short sellers must focus on precise timing and meticulous risk management. The analogy of a pilot's preflight checklist underscores the importance of preparation, as entering a trade at the wrong time can lead to significant losses.

UNDERSTANDING OPPOSING PERSPECTIVES IS KEY

Successful traders—whether long or short—benefit from understanding the mindset and strategies of their counterparts. For instance, short sellers analyze when long traders are likely to sell, while long traders recognize moments of short-selling exhaustion to capitalize on rebounds.

VOLATILITY OFFERS OPPORTUNITY AND RISK

Small-cap stocks, with their inherent volatility, present opportunities for both longs and shorts but require a deep understanding of technical patterns, fundamentals, and market dynamics to navigate effectively.

AVOID EMOTIONAL TRADING

Impulsiveness must be avoided to ensure sound trading practices. Emotional decisions often lead to mistakes, such as entering shorts too early or chasing upward momentum on longs. Experienced traders can capitalize on such missteps by sticking to their disciplined strategies.

LEVERAGING TOOLS LIKE AVWAP IMPROVES PRECISION

AVWAP provides traders with a nuanced understanding of market behavior, enabling them to identify better entry and exit points. This tool is particularly effective in detecting overextended or undervalued stocks.

ADAPTING TO DYNAMIC MARKET CONDITIONS

'Perfect-storm' scenarios, driven by factors like news, demand, and float size, highlight the need for adaptability. Traders who recognize shifting dynamics, such as demand tapering or dilution risks, are better positioned to make informed decisions.

EDUCATION AND TRANSPARENCY COMBAT MISCONCEPTIONS

Misinformation, such as the belief that short sellers manipulate prices, underscores the importance of educating traders and investors. Transparency about strategies and practices helps dispel myths and promotes a healthier trading environment. Hoarding knowledge is counterproductive and does not benefit anyone; sharing understanding and strategies uplifts the whole.

RESPECT THE BALANCE OF THE MARKET

Acknowledging the interplay between bullish and bearish trends fosters mutual respect among traders. Both roles are essential for market equilibrium and a collective effort to maintain this balance benefits all participants.

RECOGNIZE AND AVOID MANIPULATION

Traders must be vigilant about artificially driven market movements, such as those fueled by claims of 'naked short selling.' Understanding the motives behind such tactics can help traders avoid falling victim to manipulation.

THE IMPORTANCE OF COMMUNITY AND EDUCATION

Initiatives like podcasts, educational content, and in-depth research reports empower traders with knowledge and tools to navigate the market more effectively, reducing the risk of common pitfalls and improving success rates.

TIPS AND TRICKS

- **Stay in one trading lane**: It is important to focus on one particular niche. In my case, that was short selling. The human brain can become overwhelmed when considering long trading, short selling, and all that is involved with each simultaneously. If you examine the patterns of both at once, it is easy to stumble and become disorientated. Recognizing patterns in short selling paves the way for more incisive long-trading strategies. So, master one niche first and then think about pursuing the other, trading small until you have developed solid techniques and practices, using one trading lane as a building block for the other.

Chapter 12
THE WINNING MINDSET

THIS CHAPTER SUMMARIZES what it takes to succeed in the market: focusing intently on the process; journaling both mistakes and wins; entering trades judiciously, not emotionally or impetuously; and handling losses like a 'comeback wizard.' Successful trading also involves clearing your life and your thoughts of excess baggage—distractors that can potentially hamper your process. Traders must dispense with preconceived ideas and habits that can cause brain fog. Further, stay close to those who endorse, not discourage, your goals; repair/restore relationships; and clear your inner and outer space. Observe the principle of *kaizen*, discussed in Chapter 6, making incremental changes that will improve your life and your trading journey.

GOING THE DISTANCE

Success in trading, as in life, invariably involves the practice of exceptionality: going the distance and beyond to achieve the intended objective. Small wins have value too. They're good for morale—the precursors to greater achievements. Throughout the process, traders must ask themselves, 'How badly do I want to win and what am I willing to do to realize that success?'

Repeat behaviors compound over time, so I'm always hypervigilant and judicious in my actions and reactions. Some market wizards have low win rates and that's okay. These individuals maintain exceptional risk/reward ratios by minimizing losses and ensuring that their gains significantly outweigh any setbacks. This disciplined approach forms the core of their trading strategy.

FOCUS ON THE PROCESS, NOT THE WIN RATE

Percentages are just numbers. Everything hinges not on the win rate, but on the process: what goes into the trade. If a loss occurs, this does not mean that the entire practice of trading is 'bad.' The loss simply indicates that we must compartmentalize, pause, and take stock of what occurred and what we can do to learn from and improve on our strategies. Stick to the rules; apply the lessons learned; don't slack off or indulge in habits that tend to mask cognition and performance (e.g., self-medicating with alcohol).

JOURNAL WINS IN TANDEM WITH LOSSES—GO THE EXTRA MILE

I never fail to pause, take stock, and study my losses in the aftermath, so that I can convert my mistakes into inverse wins. I liken my approach to that of all-star athletes like Michael Jordan and the late Kobe Bryant—basketball legends who relentlessly honed their skills, going the extra mile, analyzing, cogitating and constantly refining their game to reach the pinnacle of success. As a result, no one could ever emulate their proficiency. Their strategies were in a league of their own.

As a corollary to the all-star-athlete mentality, it's also important to view losses as healthy and educational. Ask yourself, 'What did I do well up to this point? What caused the misstep, leaving me susceptible to loss?'

Develop a checklist of common denominators to determine whether a particular type of stock may be a red flag that could cause tremendous damage and potential financial ruin. Your entire career could be on the line. Never put yourself in that position. That is the psychology of reckless gamblers, not professional traders. The untrained temptation to short these stocks—the societal behavior that reflects conditioning to take action (i.e., enter a trade) and feel that you are being productive—will invariably arise. However, be mindful of profits from subpar trades, as they can subconsciously reinforce poor decision-making and are likely to result in significant losses over time.

Rewards that foster that kind of negative behavior cultivate bad habits, which can spiral out of control and lead to the most devastating losses. As a short seller in these scenarios, you open the door to limitless losses because theoretically the numbers can rise infinitely. This contrasts to long traders, who can lose only as much as they invest because stocks can decline to no less than zero. This does not signify, however, that long trading is more favorable than short selling. Short selling just requires greater risk management. However, short selling is a higher-probability strategy because you know the end game: the inevitable sell-off of dubious companies' stocks after significant price increases over a period of time.

For this reason, I keep myself in check and never deviate from my process. If I happen to sustain a loss, I don't blame the trading activity itself. I review my process: 'What can I do better? How can I improve my entries and exits?'

I even journal my wins to determine whether I had a sloppy entry or exit, and whether there were any trades I missed while preoccupied with another trade. In addition, I document those trades I never even took to evaluate what I could have done and how I can improve my skills moving forward. My podcasts and review videos are gauges of my process and incentivize me to keep learning and growing. These techniques serve not as publicity vehicles, but as self-development tools to enhance my trading performance.

AVOID ENTERING TRADES EMOTIONALLY OR IMPETUOUSLY

I also engage in extensive self-work and introspection, especially when evaluating losses. For example, in 2021, while I was in Puerto Rico, I communicated with experienced traders who lost multiple five-and six-figure sums when Avis Budget Group (CAR) stock surged to 800%, blindsiding short sellers and forcing them to cover their positions. This gamma squeeze (i.e., stocks that were optionable, targeted by some who—like the expert traders—anticipated its decline) caused even the most seasoned market experts to try their hand. The stock remained irrational longer than they, as short sellers, could remain solvent and they could not outlast that squeeze.

The CAR stock gamma squeeze arose in an environment in which gamma squeezes were occurring every so often, after GME and AMC had happened. It didn't follow a predictable decline pattern. Naturally, these traders were devastated, commiserated with each other, and fell prey to the negative effects of a 'misery loves company' attitude. In the aftermath of that disaster, they compared notes. I did not short the stock and hence did not experience a loss, but I felt their distress. Although I empathized with them, I knew that reciprocal consolation and commiseration are unproductive.

The best way to deal with such circumstances is to take a lesson from the loss, focus, and regroup. Consoling, attempting to escape the pain, and indulging in groupthink—"Oh, you lost on that one? I did, too. Oh, man! That was hard!"—serve no one. Instead, traders must assume the mindset of Kobe Bryant or Michael Jordan, who never wasted time grieving and commiserating. Instead, they maintained focus and came back stronger and wiser because of their setbacks.

In similar fashion, traders must concentrate and avoid a false sense of unity that misleads them into believing that their actions were acceptable. Instead of trying to improve their strategies, these individuals seek comfort from colleagues and peers. This feel-good state distracts them from building positive strategies that foster success in trading—or any high-performance endeavor.

Witnessing that unfortunate occurrence, I tried to learn from it to avoid similar events in the future myself. No one can isolate themselves from these kinds of fluctuations and unpredictability. We all become vulnerable at one point or another. However, the key is neither to dwell on the camaraderie that ensues, at times, from commiserating and handholding nor to believe for one second in the possibility that anyone is made of kryptonite.

The best anyone can do is learn from the feedback the market inevitably provides after either a win or a loss. The question in the latter case is not 'Why me?' but simply 'Why?' The market tells us what we need to do to change and adapt and what rules we need to learn and apply in the future. The market is not an echo chamber that continuously validates perspectives without challenge. On the contrary, the market does not care about feelings. Instead, it is a self-perpetuating mechanism that maintains and enhances itself through its own dynamics and feedback loops, which are inherently unpredictable. As traders, we need to adjust our strategies and adapt to the market. It is not how or what a trader feels that affects a trade, but rather how the trader reacts to wins and losses. For this reason, I document every move.

BE A COMEBACK WIZARD

The bigger the loss, the stronger the backbone needed to bear it. Large-scale traders analyze what they can do to rebound, become more adept than ever, and develop the characteristics of a comeback wizard: one who revises strategies and who analyzes wins and the qualities of those successes (were the wins well executed or sloppy and inadvertent?).

Not all losses are disasters. If we respond properly to them, they can lead to future wins. They help us hone our discipline and develop the right mental state, where we ask ourselves, 'What could I have done better?'

By contrast, when we win, we must ask, 'Is there something I missed, or did I get away with a bad habit or force a win from what could have been a loss?' And in both cases, we should also consider if we were merely trying to prove a point rather than do our best. For example, some people cannot believe that I have an over 90% win ratio and dismiss my ideas on Chinese stocks: 'I short those stocks and win.' These individuals don't understand the significance of trading longevity. They focus only on random short-term success from a few trades of Chinese stocks without anticipating the perilous ones lurking around the corner that could end their career. These traders are ticking timebombs. I know the endgame and it's just not worth it.

CLEAR OUT EXCESS BAGGAGE IN YOUR LIFE AND TRADING 'DIET'

My elimination of Chinese stocks from my trading 'diet' is a metaphor for an essential life lesson: the importance of clearing out excess baggage to achieve success in all aspects of daily living. For me, that included everything from credit card debt to toxic relationships, socialization to the detriment of a concerted focus on my objectives, overindulgence, decision fatigue, gossip, excessive thinking about trivialities, and superfluous preoccupations that waste my energy. My trading-related decision-making is on point when my life is free of such distractions. If, on the other hand, there are stressors (e.g., unnecessary arguments with others) that bleed into trading, I become subsumed by tension and am unable to concentrate on trade. That behavior can be destructive, causing short sellers to oversize into a trade and take a loss.

This chosen way of life is serious and requires dedication and persistence; it's not transitory or amenable to 'cramming,' like in college. As human beings, we are not perfect; but we can increase the odds in our favor by operating at high frequencies and aligning ourselves with our purpose. This way of thinking, acting, and reacting typically takes a long time to cultivate. It may even involve hitting rock bottom or a traumatic event, as in my case.

PAY ATTENTION TO YOUR THOUGHTS

Self-love necessarily follows from all these practices. The outcome is improved trading and better decision-making, which translates into success.

Instead of being motivated to please others, I seek to elevate myself and the circumstances at play. Others' thoughts about how I should or should not behave, both as a human being and as a trader, are irrelevant for my purposes. I am not disrespectful; I just know that if I come from the wrong place, responding to extrinsic judgments and expectations, I deviate from my purpose and my heart and mind veer in the wrong direction.

Although I cannot control the market—with its ups and downs, inevitably unpredictable odds, and squeezes—I can control myself and my surrounding conditions. There is a low barrier to market entry; but to sustain me in the long run and realize a profit, I must harness my mind and assume dominion over it.

Clicking a mouse or typing a few digits on a keyboard can determine a positive or negative outcome. Unequipped individuals will be unable to cultivate the proper mindset. Some think trading is just a hobby, and that they can make a few dollars here and there. That is not the case. Engagement is a skill that requires development and refinement over time.

If other areas of traders' lives are a mess and they click their mouse more aggressively than they should because they just want to weigh in, they will develop destructive habits. Their behavior and their lives must be controlled and organized both inside and outside the trade. When traders engage in negative or unproductive trading practices, these behaviors can be symptomatic of other troubling, unresolved aspects of their lives.

WHEN STARTING OUT, DISPENSE WITH PRECONCEIVED IDEAS AND HABITS

Since I began trading, I have sought to eliminate propensities that could cause brain fog. Trading is like six-dimensional chess, requiring the brain to operate on all cylinders. The process can be counterintuitive, and many people must unlearn everything they know or think they know about life. I, however, had nothing to unlearn, as I came in as a *tabula rasa*; I simply had to address some bad habits—and I didn't blink in doing so. A party atmosphere never served my purpose. I came in on ground zero, where there was absolutely no room to slack off. I needed all the mental prowess I could summon within me—and still do—and I must continuously cultivate a trader's mindset with razor-sharp precision and think clearly in high-pressure situations.

FREE YOUR INNER AND OUTER SPACE

Like my inner space, streamlined through self-care and awareness, my external environment must be free of physical and emotional clutter at all times. Therefore, I ensure that my surrounding space—my office and my apartment—is always meticulously clean and neat. My coffee machine is always filled with fresh water, the coffee supplemented with collagen and lion's mane (which support brain cell and neural health) to prepare me for the next trade. I take good care of my physical constitution by eating well, staying hydrated, and working out regularly at the gym.

REPAIR/RESTORE RELATIONSHIPS

My relationships are free from toxicity, allowing me to create an environment of peace, gratitude, optimal health, and happiness without drama or emotional roller coasters. If those elements of life outside the computer screen are chaotic, this can erode my mental capital. If I'm a few percentage points off my game, disaster can ensue.

SEEK OUT THOSE WHO ENERGIZE, ENCOURAGE, AND ENDORSE YOU

Along with the above philosophies and practices, I was fortunate to meet people who believed in me and not only saw me in the present but envisioned who I could become in the future. For my part, I had to choose to travel in the direction of my aspirations. To this end, I continued to study and strategize and conducted hours of podcast interviews with mentors whose knowledge bolstered and enhanced my understanding of the craft. I opened myself up to everything they had to say and pursued my life's transformation.

My evolution has involved continually surrounding myself with positivity from like-minded peers. I've learned that when trading around others, the energy is different—especially if you're an established trader. You have the data and experience, but someone can distract you by projecting their feelings about a trade, thus affecting the intended outcome. This happened to me in Puerto Rico, which was initially a great training ground; but as I grew and honed my skills, I became aware of how counterproductive such extrinsic negativity can be.

"Oh, I can't believe you shorted that! That's insane!" some traders would remark.

As I had just started out with a sizable account, feelings of insecurity would get the better of me. I covered the trade and got out, my mind racing. I remained pokerfaced, but colleagues sometimes diverted my attention and affected my trades through their unsolicited opinions on my decision-making process. I would be distracted by such comments and become more prone to hindsight bias, such that I would reflect on how I might have handled the trade had I not heard their comments. Such thoughts are unhealthy and counterproductive, often leading to regret, which can deflect from the main purpose of trading mistakes—and missteps in every sphere of life: learning from the mistake and moving forward with discipline, positivity, and determination.

One of my colleagues in Puerto Rico was an up-and-coming systematic trader at the desk across from mine. I had three brokers at the time, each with a different clearing firm and a distinct locate availability. I also had three $40,000 accounts, as I wanted to diversify, have a wider pool of short locate inventories to choose from, and have less exposure because my accounts were smaller.

"Why do you have three brokers and three accounts instead of one?" my colleague asked. "You should just have better risk management. I have automatic stop losses and a super-tight risk management approach," he remarked with an air of superiority.

"But what if there's an outlier—a black swan?" I inquired.

"Black swans are inherently unpredictable and you can't do anything about them, so you just have to have better risk management. Just have one account," my colleague insisted.

It was true. I didn't have automatic stop losses and deliberately chose to have three accounts to take smaller positions. I was in it for the long haul, with the goals of learning and ensuring longevity. I did not want to suffer a potential catastrophe with just one account.

The following year, in 2022, when ILAG came out, another trader recounted some deeply troubling news. The stock went from halt to halt and my systematic trader colleague shorted it. The stock gapped up, skipped as it halted, opened up a dollar higher, halted again, and gapped up even higher. Even with his stop losses and manual stop losses combined, my colleague could do nothing, got stuck in the stock with his one account, and lost $750,000—more than he had made in his career up to that point. I felt awful; his pain was palpable. I knew that he should not have put all his eggs in one basket. However, I never entertain an 'I told you so' mentality. That disaster could have happened to anyone, including me. I just stick to my rules, which I cultivated early on, and which are not up for rebuttal.

At some point later, I travelled to the Amalfi Coast to meet some successful traders and stayed with them in a $90 million villa. I placed a trade the morning after I arrived and exited it. A colleague who was there with me commented, "How did you do that? You held out for so long!" He repeated the same refrain at dinner that evening, referring to that trade. "I don't know how you do it. You must have ice in your veins!"

My colleague's intrusive declarations, reflecting his own insecurities, served only to reinforce my methodologies. "I love my approach; it works in the majority of cases, and I am sticking to it," I replied.

On the same trip, I was surrounded by systematic traders. The news is a big factor in my process to avoid potential outliers. So, when reports about an outbreak of monkeypox hit the headlines and some stocks in the biotech space began to move in the premarket, I was looking at the top gainers on my scanner. When I inquired about this news, my colleague, trading next to me in the villa, replied contemptuously, "You trade the news? I don't care about that. I just trade."

"Yeah, I don't care either," another retorted, trying to undermine my approach.

"I trade the news because if there is a worldwide event, I don't want to be blindsided by a black swan scenario," I explained. "I have a variety of approaches. I trade the news, I journal, I do trade reviews—I run the gamut."

These traders tried to railroad me by projecting their arrogance without respectful disagreement, probing, or conceptualization. Having diverse opinions is okay, but you must present them with deference for diverse viewpoints. Had I been a new trader, I might have been confused; but since I'm a seasoned practitioner of the trading art and science, I stick to examining the totality of the circumstances surrounding each trade.

Some traders believe they can 'crack the code' and the system will do the work for them, but they're mistaken. You can't trade effectively with that mindset in the long term—it's just not how trading works. Therefore, I adhere to my rules and discipline tenaciously, no matter what. My guide in this respect is the character of Rorschach from the *Watchmen* series, who famously said, "Never compromise. Not even in the face of Armageddon." I have that same unwavering conviction. I will never compromise; I will never stop reading the news, doing reviews, journaling, podcasting, attending conferences, associating with traders who operate at higher frequencies, adapting to the market, and constantly improving. My respectful advice to others entering the profession: don't be a Monday night quarterback. Instead, believe you're Tom Brady.

ACKNOWLEDGE THE NECESSITY OF CHANGE AND LEARN FROM FAILURES

Not everyone has a watershed opportunity or an encounter with enlightenment. People must realize there is no quick fix. The first step is to acknowledge the necessity of change and to learn from failure. Life is far from easy, but we must ask ourselves, 'How badly do I want the dream?' Test your willingness to reinvent the wheel, evolve, and achieve your full potential. Picasso may have experienced suffering during his Blue Period, but he still produced art—this was a key factor in his journey to greatness. I knew I could learn from this example and follow suit.

The beauty of the market is that there's something for everyone. You just have to carve out your own identity and stick to it. Initially, I did this by retreating into a vacuum. Then, I went public with my podcast and shared my thoughts with the global community.

In each instance, I surround myself with people who cultivate a winning mindset; I curate my environment—my physical space and inner thoughts—and avoid the toxicity of negativity that deflects from my purpose; I execute each trade with the proper risk management, so whether the result is red or green, the trade is good because I executed it meticulously and with precision. The odds are in my favor that the trade will be successful, which leads to more confidence in the next trade.

GET INTO THE GROOVE

As I get into a groove of consistent winning streaks, I reach peak performance thanks to my process: conducting in-depth trade reviews; conceptualizing with colleagues and like-minded friends; doing things I love outside of trading, such as traveling whenever I feel inclined to do so; writing this book; conducting podcasts, interviews, lectures, speeches; helping others through my trading education and experience. At this level, I feel like a piano virtuoso. I feel joyful, unafraid to trade; I savor my fresh coffee; I keep my apartment super-clean and neat; I ride the elevator to my office in the tallest building west of the Mississippi and take in the views from the 54th floor, in the best climate with the most beautiful views in the United States (in my opinion); I marvel at the cloudless blue sky while doing my Instagram Live broadcasts. I love interacting with people: "Come on! Who's in here? Ask a question! Let's conceptualize."

BECOME THE SYMPHONY CONDUCTOR OF YOUR LIFE

Today, I am honored to mentor others, share ideas, and educate people about the market through lectures and podcasts. Recently, the University of Florida invited me to be a guest lecturer at my alma mater, speaking to architecture undergraduates. The substance of that presentation follows in the next chapter.

Like trading, architecture is an art and a science. I am the embodiment of both, keenly aware that you can never tap the full extent of the universe's knowledge. To believe so would be to suffer from Faust's tragic flaw: hubris. To truly live, you must adapt to and flow with the musical symphony of life, continuously learning and evolving. The converse of this approach is stagnation and the cessation of life—and I don't want any part of that.

Over time, I came to understand that if I was to succeed, my initial 'fight-or-flight' trading behavior was unsustainable. By seeking knowledge and focusing on discipline and conditioning, I broke through the veil of vulnerability to envision myself as a $1 million trader. That was not just an illusory wish, but an imminent reality. When 'seeing' my future self in my mind's eye, I went for the quantum leap, honing my process in every waking moment, making it as rigorous, meticulous, and foolproof as I could in a counterintuitive environment like the market. I wasn't playing around; my transformation was not a joke. I wanted to emulate gurus (as opposed to 'furus'—fake would-be mentors with nothing to offer). I emulated excellence not only in the world of trading but in life—like a musical virtuoso, the conductor of my life's symphony. I had to adjust my carriage, conduct, thinking, and general awareness of myself and my daily living habits—my lifestyle, dietary practices, living conditions (i.e., cleanliness and decluttering of my environment), thought processes, and how they affect my trades.

As I evolved, I also discovered that living within my own four walls was not enough; I had to go out and conceptualize with those who thought, breathed, and practically consumed stocks. As I learned and listened, I increased my probability of achieving greater success. That's what I hope to do for others like me who wish to commit to trading as an art and a profession: to guide them toward greater odds of success by using the right strategies and methodologies, nurturing a winning mindset, and ultimately developing a universal trading model that effectively makes the mid-to-high 90% failure ratio a thing of the past.

LESSONS LEARNED

MAINTAIN DISCIPLINE AT ALL TIMES

Ensure your gains outweigh your setbacks by applying a disciplined approach, as discussed throughout this book.

Compete against your former self, not against others.

It is fruitless to compete with others. Doing so gives rise to an infinite cycle of failure. As renowned American basketball and baseball player Michael Jordan once noted, "I don't compete with other people … I compete with what I'm capable of." When you compete with your former self—the person you were yesterday—you set yourself up for consistent self-improvement, which leads to a pattern of success: a snowball effect that allows you to surpass all your goals.

PROCESS SUPERSEDES WIN RATE

Don't try to force wins. Just follow your plan and focus on your best execution.

HEED THE KNOWLEDGE IN THIS BOOK

Retail traders have access to limited information. Successful traders often hoard knowledge because they fear eroding their edge. The instructions imparted in this book and at the Friendly Bear University make that knowledge accessible. I have become the mentor I always sought to learn from. My goal in mentoring was to share my knowledge and experience with others so that they have an equal opportunity to succeed in trading. I advise my readers to revisit the text—the material is not intended to be read once but digested over the long term.

COMMIT TO A WINNING MINDSET

Success—personal and professional—is not accidental but the result of deliberate effort, unwavering conviction, and consistent practice. Visualizing future success and embodying the qualities necessary to achieve it are central to realizing one's aspirations.

TIPS AND TRICKS

- **Do not be discouraged by losses**: Losses highlight your blind spots and force you to become better.
- **Be internally competitive**: Focus on improving yourself each day. Everyone has different circumstances prevailing in their lives. Avoid comparison—that is the best method for performing at your optimum.
- **Don't listen to negative commentary about your chosen profession**: What matters is your belief in yourself; and in the final analysis, your success will speak for itself.
- **Beware of your lifestyle**: Take note of behaviors and actions outside of trading that could affect your performance negatively (e.g., obvious

vices such as smoking and drinking, or attitudinal vices such as road rage or sloppy habits pertaining to your dress or within your home).

- **Learn always**: Read voraciously and consume content such as *The Friendly Bear* podcast instead of binge-streaming TV series or movies.
- **Be selective about your associations with other traders**: Unfortunately, most traders lose and are not serious about the trading discipline.

Chapter 13

THE LIMITLESS CLUB

Trading is counterintuitive. You must do the opposite of what human nature dictates. Meticulousness and precision mitigate the unexpected. Be proactive but cautious. If you look to trading to resolve your financial woes, that is a recipe for disaster. New and aspiring traders don't want to acknowledge this fact. The truth sometimes runs counter to what people wish to hear, but facing up to reality always saves time and suffering in the long term. Looking back, I wish I'd had someone to guide and reassure me that I had chosen the right path. Since I didn't have that support, I took a shot in the dark.

When I review my podcasts from 2021 to 2022, I'm struck by how different I was then. I don't even recognize my former self. But I realize now that, just as forces change in the trading world, so must the individual trader. I experienced a metamorphosis and broke out of the mold. It became clear to me that I was not simply meant to be a trader sitting behind four screens in an office, but a change agent capable of sharing my knowledge.

TRADE FOR THE RIGHT REASONS

Becoming a trader requires a commitment to entrepreneurship, just as you would devote your time to any other profession. Clear your headspace, address your financial problems, and get your life in order before even attempting to enter a trade. Pay the minimums on your credit cards, repair your relationships (including with your landlord/lady), and eliminate physical and emotional chaos and drama in your environment. This will free up your mental capital to trade sensibly. Remember that a strategy for making massive amounts to pay off rent and credit card debt does not exist and will not magically appear from the ether. You (and only you) are the catalyst for extricating yourself from life's messes. If you enter trades with money in mind, you will make the wrong decisions. Your thinking must be incisive. When a stock goes against them, impetuous traders—both long and short—chase it up and down and don't cut their losses. You must accept defeat. If your outer world is in shambles, that nightmare will obscure your vision.

DEVASTATING LOSSES FROM HOBBY TRADING

The same principles apply to trading as a hobby. If you dabble in the discipline, you must be aware that painful, demoralizing setbacks are inevitable and breakeven is a positive. If you have another career, loss is more difficult to fathom and accept because you might have more impetus to quit—you have a fallback in your life. However, you just have to keep going and cultivate an attitude of resilience and commitment to learning. Consider the following hypothetical: a successful engineer sets aside $30,000 to invest in trading. He is excited at the prospect of learning a new skill and is ideally positioned to flourish as a trader: he pays his bills on time, he has family support, and his life is in order. In other words, he has set the stage. "I have nothing to lose, even if this $30,000 disappears. I will take a year, try it out, and see what happens."

As a responsible, intelligent person, the engineer does everything right. For two months, he reads books, watches trading videos and podcasts, and observes the candlestick patterns assiduously and deliberately without sizing up into trades too early. He does well, neither winning nor losing. Then suddenly, greed slips in and he forgets his promise to himself about taking things step by step. He oversizes into plays and things go fine for a while. He even has a couple of wins. But then, all at once, he loses $10,000 in one trade. "I'll try one more time," he tells himself, losing another $2,000. This error is, sadly, all too common. In poker, there's a common adage: 'Losses come in pairs.' The statement stems from people's tendency to chase their initial losses, often leading to more aggressive decisions in their selectivity and position sizing. Unfortunately, this aggression often does not align with their usual strategy, increasing the likelihood of another significant loss. For our engineer, discouragement sets in: predictably, the $10,000-plus loss is devastating, notwithstanding his initial nonchalance and purportedly low expectations. That's because money is hard-earned over time.

A word to the wise

In the stock market, traders make and lose money in seconds or milliseconds. Successful traders build their accounts gradually, practicing tight risk management to ensure that early losses are low. With profitable strategies and consistency, you can grow your account and create a buffer between real-world and stock market-earned money. Once you carefully distinguish between the two, you can trade with a clearer focus.

TRUE GRIT

A dual career as described in the above hypothetical (and successful trading in general) is possible only if you're willing to train like Rocky Balboa, with an unswerving commitment to achieving championship status. Rocky's drill of chasing chickens, inspired by his coach, epitomizes the mental fortitude and resilience of someone willing to hone their creativity and skill and translate them into ultimate success. Persistence and tenacity are key to Rocky's process as he trains in the cold snow and sprints up the steps of the Philadelphia Museum of Art—an iconic moment in film history, depicting the grit required to transform an underdog into a champion who takes their rightful place in the ring, regardless of the outcome.

FAILURE TEACHES US LIFE LESSONS

Learning from failure is a positive; but if you give up without learning from your mistakes, failure becomes decisive and permanent. You can head out for a walk in the park to regroup, but you must then return and have a plan. Strategize, study more, journal more. There is no escape route. Ask yourself, 'Why am I in this position, and what can I do—other than back out—to rectify the mistake and recover?' There is no shame in losing; but quitting signifies inevitable, prolonged inertia and a sense of defeat that serves no one and nothing.

ADMIT YOUR LACK OF KNOWLEDGE

The beauty of trading lies in its inherent unpredictability and the corresponding potential for market explorers and wizards alike to learn constantly. The process never ends. That should not frighten you; it should make you hypervigilant and eager. Just when you feel you know everything, the market brings you down to earth, back to reality, where we all belong.

Our destinies hinge on our self-belief and willingness to do the hard work. Once you achieve 'championship status,' things do not end there. On the contrary, you reach a new beginning. I am no exception. I learn and grow every day. As I mentioned before, a mindset that insists you know everything is deceptive—nothing but hubris.

Some people, especially those who listen to my podcast or hear me speak, don't understand when I say that I have more to learn. "You know everything!" they insist. They know some of my story: how many hours I've put in, books I've read, videos I've watched, etc.

I'm flattered by this claim, but the perception that I have somehow acquired all knowledge is simply untrue. Like everyone, I am a work in progress.

AN ADVANCED CONCEPT: USING WARRANTS AS A HEDGE TO SHORT STOCKS

For example, I am now learning about the advantages for warrant holders of using their warrants as a hedge to short their own stock. They can do so repeatedly instead of exercising their warrants just once. This is a high-level concept I could not even begin to process at the novice level.

Here's how it works: warrants provide warrant holders with a one-time opportunity to profit if the stock price exceeds the strike price (i.e., the predetermined price at which a holder buys or sells a company's stock). However, warrant holders can increase their profit opportunities by shorting the stock, which they can do repeatedly, taking their profit more than once when they use their warrants against their short position. Additionally, warrants can serve as a hedge, allowing investors to buy back the stock by covering their short position to exercise the warrant as it rises. This process offsets the losses incurred from the short position and increases the potential to break even in volatile markets.

Don't worry if the above explanation boggles your mind. It's supposed to—especially for those new to day trading—because there's always more to learn.

COMPLACENCY: THE ENEMY OF SUCCESS

Long-term success is possible in a very real sense. Starting out with nothing can be an incentive to keep going, as was the case for me. I frontloaded all my knowledge, gaining traction with every breath. I didn't have the luxury of becoming an intern at a prestigious securities firm, working 20 hours a day; I didn't have the benefit of amassing knowledge in the same way interns learn at big investment banks, gaining profitability within two or three years. They have access to top-tier knowledge and the world's best available resources at their fingertips. I followed their trajectory, despite the obstacles, and became an autodidact, starting out from zero. I persisted in the game on my own because I had everything and nothing to lose; and I did so long enough to learn the ups and downs and realize that loss is fundamentally healthy. If you never experience loss, you have nowhere to go. There's a danger in that: complacency is the enemy of success.

BASIC BUILDING BLOCKS FOR ACHIEVEMENT

The pertinent questions are: 'How badly do you want to succeed in trading and how high is your pain tolerance?' People always tell me I am resilient and ask, 'How did you do it?' I couldn't stop to analyze my decision or my approach, as I placed myself on the fast track to self-actualization. I went from studying architecture to becoming the architect of my own fate; and in the process, I had to do things right the first time. There were no do-overs—I had burned the boats. So, I had to learn the basics:

- discipline;
- 10,000 hours of study time; and
- preparedness to lose.

With little money to my name, I had a greater chance of succeeding in the small-cap space. So, in hindsight, what seemed like a liability (being under the PDT rule) when I began turned out to be a blessing, enabling me to practice the necessary small-sizing technique that gave me staying power. Who knows what might have happened had I had a larger account! I could have lost everything, thinking there might be a way out of the maze—and I could not afford that mindset or that option.

HUMILITY AND EQUILIBRIUM

Finally, it's essential to remain humble and emotionally stable. As I walk down the streets of Los Angeles, I'm reminded of the early days when I started from the ground up—quite literally. As I write, I sit in the same office—a constant reminder of my former novice status, the grind I faced back then, and the relentless hard work I will always embrace. The strength I developed from that experience evokes the go-getter in me—a trait I can summon at any time. I will never stop. I vividly recall the self-imposed sleepless nights on my office floor; or the shaven-head guy who showered on Skid Row, cloistering himself away from life to learn a discipline about which he once knew nothing. The floor beneath my feet, here in my 'fortress of solitude,' echoes the memory of forced wakefulness as I anticipated preparation for the premarket. My painting of the burning of the boats reminds me of my unflinching determination to leave everything behind, compelling me to become the man I am today.

THOUGHTS ARE MANIFESTATIONS OF INTENTION

As I look around me in downtown Los Angeles, I see polar opposites: Skid Row and the financial district; a panoply of beautiful sights, from the vibrant street art to the shimmering skyscrapers and bustling financial district. Together, these neighborhoods form a stunning, sometimes jarring, mosaic of humanity, highlighting the extremes of wealth and poverty, hope and despair, that exist within a single urban landscape. We all belong, and we all make choices. Our fate depends on where we, as individuals, direct our intention.

In which direction do *you* want to go? Whatever path you choose, it is important to remember the Huna (Hawaiian) philosophical affirmation, 'Energy flows where attention goes.' You must be careful about where you focus your thoughts, because your thoughts inevitably become manifestations of intention. In other words, a different life is just a few decisions away. Develop a skill; cultivate an aptitude; proactively find solutions by changing your mindset in the land of opportunity—the ultimate fertile ground for self-determination and success.

I am beyond grateful for my incisive decision-making and the opportunities that have risen to meet me along the way. I'm also immensely thankful for the ability to envision and create a reality of my own imagining as the founder of the Friendly Bear University. I strive to teach, inspire, and educate those who—like me—are starting out as blank slates.

In the process, I want to vanquish the mid-to-high 90% failure rate in the trading discipline by practicing and demonstrating the significance of self-belief, hard work, tenacity, focus and continuous learning—a journey not about wins but sustained resilience, personal growth, and financial freedom. I'm up for the challenge. Are you?

LESSONS LEARNED

TRADING IS COUNTERINTUITIVE

Success in trading requires a mindset that defies human nature. Emotional decisions lead to mistakes; meticulous preparation and a clear strategy are essential. Trading is not a quick fix for financial problems but a disciplined commitment to long-term growth.

PREPARATION IS KEY

Before entering the trading discipline with a view to pursuing it as a career, ensure your personal life is in order. Address financial, emotional, and relational issues to free up mental space for the complexities of trading. Chaos in your personal environment inevitably spills into your trading decisions.

LOSSES ARE INEVITABLE AND EDUCATIONAL

Setbacks are a natural part of trading. Learning from losses, rather than being defeated by them, builds resilience and fosters growth. Breakeven, particularly for beginners, is a milestone that signals progress.

COMPLACENCY IS DANGEROUS

Constant learning and adaptation are non-negotiable in trading. The market is ever-changing and those who stop evolving risk stagnation or failure. Stay curious, vigilant, and humble, recognizing that mastery is a continuous process.

PERSISTENCE AND TENACITY PAY OFF

Achieving trading success is akin to rigorous athletic training—it requires relentless effort, resilience, and a high pain tolerance. The journey demands grit and perseverance, even in the face of significant challenges.

SUCCESS IS ROOTED IN THE BASICS

Building a solid foundation—discipline, extensive study, and small-scale, calculated practice—is essential. Starting small allows for sustainable growth and minimizes the risk of catastrophic losses.

SELF-BELIEF DRIVES ACHIEVEMENT

The belief in one's ability to overcome obstacles and create opportunities is critical. Visualizing success, combined with focused action, transforms intention into reality. This mindset shift empowers traders to navigate the highs and lows of navigating the market.

STAY HUMBLE AND BALANCED

Even as you achieve success, maintaining humility and emotional equilibrium is vital. Success is not a final destination but the beginning of new challenges and opportunities for growth.

FAILURE IS A TEACHING EXPERIENCE

Failures, when approached constructively, offer invaluable lessons that lead to eventual success. Quitting prematurely, without reflection or adaptation, transforms failure into a self-fulfilling prophecy.

THOUGHTS SHAPE REALITY

A focused, intentional mindset is the cornerstone of success. Directing your focus toward growth and opportunity manifests positive outcomes. Success begins with disciplined thinking and strategic decision-making.

IMPACT BEYOND INDIVIDUAL SUCCESS

True fulfillment comes from sharing knowledge and uplifting others. By helping aspiring traders avoid common pitfalls, you create a legacy of empowerment, reducing the failure rate and fostering a community of informed, resilient traders.

A word to the wise

If you go long and short at the same time, this is a net zero that cancels out. If the stock squeezes, warrant holders can exercise their warrants, which negates or reduces a loss.

The holders can only exercise the warrants once for a profit; but if they short them, they can cover and re-short as many times as they wish. The hedging strategy is high level, not for beginners. However, there is always something to learn, improve, and reach for as you grow your account. Beginners just have to stay alive and not dive in too deeply. You can become profitable and make a solid career without having this information. Knowledge can be incrementally acquired as you develop strategies and gain experience, never slacking in the learning process. You will figure out the nuances as you go. Don't allow the 'big picture' to overwhelm you—that is the key to longevity in the industry.

TIPS AND TRICKS

Warrants are owned both by individuals and by small to large funds that can be optimized with algorithms and actively trade in the small-cap arena. When these sophisticated players short the stock below their warrant prices, the warrants act as a hedge. In Dilution Tracker, there is a section next to the current warrants on the stock's profile page that displays the warrant holders. These individuals don't invest in the companies and funds; they trade them and short the stock as well. When warrant holders exercise their warrants, the company receives the cash.

GLOSSARY

Please note that the following list is not exhaustive. It contains and clarifies terms and phrases mentioned specifically in the foregoing text.

A

Algorithm: A mechanistic set of predefined rules and calculations designed to execute trades automatically based on specific market criteria.

Anchored volume-weighted average price (AVWAP): A modified version of volume-weighted average price allowing traders to choose a starting point, such as a major event, for analyzing price trends relative to key moments.

AskEdgar: Utilizes AI to simplify the research process for Securities and Exchange Commission filings.

Asset: Any resource or item of value that can be traded, invested in, or held with the expectation of generating a return or increasing in value. Assets are the underlying items being bought or sold in financial markets.

B

Bag-holders: Investors holding onto losing stocks with little hope of recovery.

Bear market: A market characterized by prolonged price declines, favorable for short sellers.

Bid-ask: The difference between the highest price a buyer is willing to pay (bid) and the lowest price a seller will accept (ask).

Billionaire plays: Investment strategies driven by billionaire announcements of a stake in a company or their association with a major headline or catalyst. These moves often generate significant market excitement and trading volume, creating potential opportunities for strategic positioning.

Biotech stocks: Stocks of biotechnology companies, often highly volatile due to drug approvals or failures.

Black swan events: Rare and unpredictable events causing major market disruptions.

Blow-off top: A rapid price surge followed by a sharp reversal, signaling the end of an uptrend.

Blue-chip stocks: Shares of well-established, financially sound companies with a reliable track record.

Boiler rooms: High-pressure sales environments promoting dubious stocks, often linked to dubious schemes, such as pump-and-dump operations, market manipulation, and deceptive practices targeting unsophisticated investors.

Borrow-fee rate: The overnight rate for holding shorts overnight. This rate fluctuates constantly based on supply and demand of short sellers wanting to short a stock and is a way to reverse-engineer short interest intraday.

Bubble: A market condition in which asset prices exceed intrinsic value, often followed by a sharp correction.

Bullish market: A market with rising prices, benefiting long traders.

Buying opportunity: Favorable conditions for purchasing undervalued assets.

Broker: An intermediary who facilitates trades for investors and lends shares for short selling.

C

Candlestick patterns: Visual representations of price movement within a specified time frame, used in technical analysis.

Capitulation: When investors sell en masse after prolonged losses, often creating opportunities for short sellers.

Catalysts: Events or news that significantly influences market prices.

Contrast bias: A cognitive bias that occurs when an individual evaluates or judges something in comparison to something else rather than on its own merits.

D

Day trading: Buying and selling securities within a single trading day.

Delisting: Removal of a company's stock from an exchange, often causing price drops.

Demand: The desire of buyers in the market, impacting price movements.

Dilution: The reduction in ownership percentage caused by issuing additional shares.

Dilution Tracker: Software monitoring share dilution and its effects on stock price.

Direct access brokers: Brokers offering fast execution and advanced trading tools for active traders.

Dubious stocks: Companies that engage in questionable practices and never amount to anything.

F

Fear of missing out (FOMO): An emotional response, leading traders to make impulsive decisions to avoid missing potential profits.

Filings: Official documents submitted by companies to regulatory bodies, such as earnings reports.

Financial Industry Regulatory Authority (FINRA): A regulatory body overseeing broker-dealer firms and protecting investors.

First red day: The first day of price decline after a stock has been on an exponential upward trend.

Form 13G filing: Discloses ownership of more than 5% of a publicly owned company.

Furus: Fake gurus—influential, inauthentic traders who use the lure of materialism and lifestyle to hold themselves out as mentors. They sell a dream, rather than offer valuable, workable insight and education. Beware!

Futures brokerages: Firms facilitating the trading of futures contracts.

G

Gap-up: A sharp price increase between a stock's previous close and the next day's opening price.

H

Hedge: A strategy used to reduce or offset investment risks.

Herd mentality: The tendency for traders to follow the majority, often leading to overvaluation or bubbles.

High-odds strategy: A trading plan with a high probability of success.

Historical charts: Visual data showing past price movements to analyze trends.

I

Institutional ownership: The percentage of a company's stock held by large institutions, affecting liquidity and volatility.

Interactive brokers: Popular trading brokerages offering diverse markets and low fees.

L

Level 2, bid and ask: Market depth data showing the highest bids and lowest asks for a security.

Liquidity: How easily and quickly shares can be bought or sold in the market without significantly affecting the stock's price, typically measured by trading volume and bid-ask spreads.

Locate fees: Fees short sellers pay to locate shares for borrowing to short intraday.

Long trading: Buying stocks with the expectation of price increases.

M

Manipulation: Deliberate attempts to influence market prices unfairly.

Market cap: The total market value of a company's outstanding shares.

Market open: The start of the trading day, 9:30 a.m. EST.

N

Naked short selling: The illegal practice of short selling shares without borrowing them.

Nano float: Stocks with under 1 million shares available to trade publicly.

Nasdaq: A major U.S. stock exchange known for its tech-focused listings.

New York Stock Exchange (NYSE): A leading global exchange known for more stringent listing requirements.

O

Options: Financial derivatives giving the right, but not the obligation, to buy or sell an asset at a specific price within a certain time period.

Outlier: A data point significantly deviating from others, impacting trading strategies.

Overvaluation: When a stock's market price exceeds its intrinsic value.

P

Paid pump promotion: Promotional campaigns designed to inflate stock prices artificially.

Pattern day trade (PDT) rule: A regulation requiring a limitation on how often a trader can execute a trade.

Percentage increase intraday: The percentage change in a stock's price within a single trading day.

Premarket: Trading activity occurring before the regular market session.

Price action: The movement of a stock's price over time.

Price deviations: Variations in price from expected levels.

Price movements: The changes in a stock's price within a time frame.

Price spikes: Sudden and sharp increases in price.

Pump-and-dump schemes: Schemes where prices are artificially inflated and then sold off by insiders.

Q

Qualitative analysis: Assessing a company's value based on intangible factors like management quality.

Quantitative analysis: Using numerical data to evaluate investments.

R

Reverse split: Consolidating shares to reduce the number of outstanding shares and increase the stock price.

S

Securities and Exchange Commission (SEC) filings: Publicly available documents filed with the SEC.

Short selling: A trading strategy in which an investor borrows shares of a stock or other asset from a broker and sells them on the open market, with the intention of buying them back later at a lower price.

Sizing: Determining the appropriate number of shares for a trade.

Small caps: Companies with a market cap between $250 million and $2 billion.

Speculation: High-risk trading based on anticipated market movements.

Squeeze (short squeeze): A sharp price increase forcing short sellers to cover their positions.

Stocks: Financial instruments (shares) that represent ownership in a company.

Supply: The availability of shares for trading.

Swing trading: A trading strategy that allows traders to capitalize on price swings in financial markets. Traders hold positions for a few days to a few weeks, exploiting market volatility and trends. Unlike day trading, which involves closing positions within the same trading day, swing trading allows for trades to remain open overnight, requiring a slightly longer time horizon.

Sympathy plays: Trades in stocks related to a primary mover in the same industry.

T

Technical analysis: Using charts and patterns to predict price movements.

Trade Ideas: Scanning software used to identify trading opportunities in real-time.

Tulip Mania: A historical market bubble and crash in the Netherlands in the 17th century.

V

Volatility: The degree of price variation within a market or security.

Volume: The number of shares traded during a specific period.

Volume-weighted average price (VWAP): A measure of a stock's average price over a day based on volume and price.

W

Warrants: Financial instruments giving the right to buy a company's stock at a specific price.

Wash trading: A manipulative practice involving buying and selling the same security to create artificial market activity.

Win ratio: The percentage of successful trades compared to total trades made.

ABOUT THE AUTHOR

DAVID CAPABLANCA is an expert short seller, investment educator, and podcast host on a mission to end predatory Wall Street behavior and teach everyday people how to gain financial freedom. As a seven-figure short trader with a verified win ratio of over 90%, he created *The Friendly Bear* podcast to give bear market players a platform for discourse.

Capablanca also founded the Friendly Bear University, which trains members in investment strategies and skills. His aim: to revolutionize traders' approach to financial markets, vanquish the failure rate, and unlock a path to personal and professional fulfillment, competence, and success.

In 2009, Capablanca graduated *cum laude* from the University of Florida, after studying in Paris, France and Vicenza, Italy for extended periods.

While attending UCLA's master's program in architecture, Capablanca was diagnosed with a brain tumor. He not only triumphed over his illness but emerged with a renewed sense of purpose. He worked tirelessly to complete his studies and achieve optimum health. During his final year at UCLA, he studied with Pritzker Prize-winning architect Thom Mayne and took part in his Suprastudio.

Capablanca's graduate studies and medical bills left him with significant debt and limited prospects in a low-paying entry-level architecture position. So, he redirected his goals and devoted his life to learning the underpinnings of trading and mastering the stock market (specifically, short selling) to pay off his debts and live his best life. Central to his motivation is a desire to help others do the same.

To his eclectic list of interests and accomplishments, Capablanca adds his travels to Haiti and Indonesia to lead teams in reconstructing schools after natural disasters with the nonprofit AllHandsandHearts.org.

Capablanca still has a love of architecture and keeps up with the latest trends, technology, and history of architecture-related topics. In his spare time, he volunteers at the Hollyhock House, designed by Frank Lloyd Wright. He is based in Los Angeles.